Legal Drafting

Practical Exercises
and
Problem Materials

By
Thomas R. Haggard

David W. Robinson Professor of Law
University of South Carolina School of Law

AMERICAN CASEBOOK SERIES®

WEST GROUP

ST. PAUL, MINN., 1999

610 Opperman Drive
P.O. Box 64526
St. Paul, MN 55164–0526
1–800–328–9352

Printed in the United States of America

ISBN 0–314–23362–8

TEXT IS PRINTED ON 10% POST CONSUMER RECYCLED PAPER

Dedicated To My Wife

Nell,

With Love and Admiration

PREFACE

This is not a textbook *about* legal drafting. It contains no instruction on the process, techniques, or skills of the drafting art. Presumably, you have been assigned another text covering those matters. The purpose of this book, rather, is to provide you with the opportunity to take what you have learned in the abstract and put it into practice.

The exercises in Part I do this in small, incremental steps, allowing you to focus on one particular aspect at a time -- without worrying about creating a complete and well-drafted document all at once. These exercises contain a reference to the pages in two widely used drafting texts that discuss the specific topic of that exercise. They are as follows:

> Thomas R. Haggard, *Legal Drafting in a Nutshell* (1996) (cited as "Haggard").
>
> Barbara Child, *Drafting Legal Documents--Principles and Practices* (2d ed. 1992) (cited as "Child").

Do not be surprised if your instructor assigns these exercises in a different order. I often do so myself.

The exercises in Part II then enable you to bring it all together and to produce a variety of documents, some *from scratch* and others from existing albeit badly drafted documents.

This is also not a book on substantive law. It will not make you a fully competent drafter in any particular field. On the other hand, legal drafting obviously cannot be done in a complete substantive-law vacuum. Some of the exercises, thus, will contain information about the relevant substantive law and the matters that should be dealt with in a particular type of document. The information, however, is of secondary importance, it does not purport to be comprehensive with respect to any given topic, and it may not even be the controlling law in your jurisdiction. Its only purpose is to give you a typical substantive law context within which to draft a document. Once you have mastered the techniques of drafting, then you can marry those techniques to *whatever* substantive law is relevant to the document you have been asked to draft.

Similarly, the statutory analysis and drafting exercises do not assume that you are going to become a legislative drafter. The skills and techniques that they require of you are essentially fungible; you can use them just as effectively when analyzing, redrafting, or drafting complex private-law documents.

Most of the exercises in this book have been *field tested* on my own students. I want to thank them for their patience, criticisms, and suggestions.

I hope you enjoy the exercises. I had a great deal of fun creating them. And if you have any criticisms or suggestions, I welcome them. Feel free to contact me here at the University of South Carolina School of Law, Columbia, SC 29208, or by e-mail at tom@law.law.sc.edu.

Thomas R. Haggard
Lake Wateree, SC
Summer 1998

TABLE OF CONTENTS

Page

Legal Drafting

Practical Exercises
and
Problem Materials

PART I.

Exercise 1: Getting Started

Legal drafting does not begin with writing. It begins with gathering and evaluating information. Specifically, the drafter must determine what the client's objectives are, who will use the document and for what purposes, and the factual and legal context within which the document will operate. *See* Haggard 36-50; Child 288-94.

1. Assume that a client has asked you to draft the following documents. You have scheduled a meeting to discuss the matter. The first thing you will want to know, of course, is why the client wants this document. Consider all of the possible objectives the client might have and how each of these objectives would affect the substance of the document.

a. A state statute regulating personal watercraft or *jet boats*.

b. A provision prohibiting *moonlighting* that will be incorporated into an employee handbook. [Since a handbook is likely to be construed as having contractual significance, its provisions must be drafted with the same care that would be used when drafting any other contract.]

2. Now evaluate these possible objectives from the perspective of other parties to the transaction, prior transactions between these parties, the scope of the anticipated use, and the possibility of conflict if the client is a multiple entity.

3. Identify everyone, other than the immediate parties, who might have to deal with these documents and consider how their characteristics might affect the drafting process.

4. Concisely describe what you would look for when exploring the legal and factual context within which these documents will operate.

Exercise 2: Drafting Within the Law

Some drafted documents are subject to complex and numerous legal constraints -- corporate security and estate planning documents, for example. Others are subject only to simple common law rules, like those affecting the formation and validity of a contract. *See* Haggard 51-63.

The document in this exercise is subject to legal constraints of intermediate numerosity and complexity.

A client wants you to draft a waiver of age discrimination claims that departing employees will be asked to sign. These waivers are regulated by the Older Workers Benefit Protection Act, 29 U.S.C. § 626(f), amending the Age Discrimination in Employment Act, 29 U.S.C. §§ 621-634. Prepare a legal checklist based on the provisions of this statute, the EEOC Regulations, and some relevant cases.

29 U.S.C. § 626(f):

(1) An individual may not waive any right or claim under this Act unless the waiver is knowing and voluntary. Except as provided in paragraph (2), a waiver may not be considered knowing and voluntary unless at a minimum —

(A) the waiver is part of an agreement between the individual and the employer that is written in a manner calculated to be understood by such individual, or by the average individual eligible to participate;

(B) the wavier specifically refers to rights or claims arising under this Act;

(C) the individual does not waive rights or claims that may arise after the date the waiver is executed;

(D) the individual waives rights or claims only in exchange for consideration in addition to anything of value to which the individual already is entitled;

(E) the individual is advised in writing to consult with an attorney prior to executing the agreement;

(F)(i) the individual is given a period of at least 21 days within which to consider the agreement; or

(ii) if a waiver is requested in connection with an exit incentive or other employment termination program offered to a group or class of employees, the individual is given a period of at least 45 days within which to consider the agreement;

(G) the agreement provides that for a period of at least 7 days following the execution of such agreement, the individual may revoke the agreement, and the agreement shall not become effective or enforceable until the revocation period has expired;

(H) if a wavier is requested in connection with an exit incentive or other employment termination program offered to a group or class of employees, the employer (at the commencement of the period specified in subparagraph (F)) informs the individual in writing in a manner calculated to be understood by the average individual eligible to participate, as to —

(i) any class, unit, or group of individuals covered by such program, any eligibility factors for such program, and any time limits applicable to such program; and

(ii) the job titles and ages of all individuals eligible or selected for the program, and the ages of all individuals in the same job classification or organizational unit who are not eligible or selected for the program.

(2) A waiver in settlement of a charge filed with the Equal Employment Opportunity Commission, or an action filed in court by the individual or the individual's representative, alleging age discrimination of a kind prohibited under section 4 or 15 may not be considered knowing and voluntary unless at a minimum —

(A) subparagraphs (A) through (E) of paragraph (1) have been met; and

(B) the individual is given a reasonable period of time within which to consider the settlement agreement.

Equal Employment Opportunity Commission, 29 C.F.R. § 1625.22:

. . . .

(b) Wording of Waiver Agreements

. . . .

(3) Waiver agreements must be drafted in plain language geared to the level of understanding of the individual party to the agreement or individuals eligible to participate. Employers should take into account such factors as the level of comprehension and education of typical participants. Consideration of these factors usually will require the limitation or elimination of technical jargon and of long, complex sentences.

. . . .

(6) [T]he waiver agreement must refer to the Age Discrimination in Employment Act (ADEA) by name in connection with the waiver.

. . . .

(e) Time Periods.

. . . .

(5) The 7 day revocation period cannot be shortened by the parties, by agreement or otherwise.

(6) An employee may sign a release prior to the end of the 21 or 45 day time period, thereby commencing the mandatory 7 day revocation period. This is permissible as long as the employee's decision to accept such shortening of time is knowing and voluntary and is not induced by the employer through fraud, misrepresentation, a threat to withdraw or alter the offer prior to the expiration of the 21 or 45 day time period, or by providing different terms to employees who sign the release prior to the expiration of such time period.

Griffin v. Kraft General Foods, Inc., 62 F.2d 368 (11th Cir. 1995):

. . . .

2. Nonstatutory Factors Showing That the Waiver Was Not "Knowing and Voluntary"

The employees contend that the district court should have considered the "totality of the circumstances," in addition to the explicit OWBPA requirements, to determine if their waiver of ADEA rights was "knowing and voluntary." Prior to the OWBPA's enactment, a federal common-law rule based on the ADEA had emerged permitting ADEA waivers only if they were knowing and voluntary, as determined by an open-ended list of factors. . . . . The OWBPA's language and legislative history strongly support the plaintiffs' contention that the nonstatutory circumstances considered in

> these cases survive the enactment of the OWBPA. . . .

Pierce v. Atchison, Topeka & Santa Fe Ry. Co., 65 F.3d 562 (7th Cir. 1995):

> . . . .
>
> Like the other circuits that currently employ the federal totality approach, a court should look to a number of factors to assess the validity of a particular release, including, but not limited to: (1) the employee's education and business experience; (2) the employee's input in negotiating the terms of the settlement; (3) the clarity of the agreement; (4) the amount of time the employee had for deliberation before signing the release; (5) whether the employee actually read the release and considered its terms before signing it; (6) whether the employee was represented by counsel or consulted with an attorney; (7) whether the consideration given in exchange for the waiver exceeded the benefits to which the employee was already entitled by contract or law; and (8) whether the employee's release was induced by improper conduct on the defendant's part. . . .

Wamsley v. Champlin Ref. & Chem., Inc., 11 F.3d 534 (5th Cir. 1993):

> . . . .
>
> In November and December, Champlin informed Appellants that they were

among the employees who were going to be "let go." Champlin provided them with a "Notice Pertaining to Release of Claims" document and a "Release of Claims" agreement. The notice included the following provision:

> Although you may execute the Release of Claims as soon as you wish, you also may take up to 45 days from your receipt of the Release of Claims to consider it. Your decision to execute the Release of Claims and accept benefits under the Termination Pay Plan will be revocable for seven days after execution, and no payment of termination pay will be made until that period has expired. Therefore, to be able to provide your termination pay to you not later than five business days after the termination of your employment, the Company must receive your executed Release of Claims at least seven days before that payment date.

The release provided for Appellants' waiver of any action or claim against Champlin and "its successors, assigns, [and] affiliates," "relating to or arising out of [their] employment with [Champlin] . . . or the termination of such employment, including but not limited to, claims for . . . age discrimination under . . . the Age Discrimination in Employment Act of 1967." The release made clear that the benefits to be paid under the Plan constituted the consideration for the release.

. . . .

Appellants responded to Champlin's motion and proof by tendering affidavits in which each swore to facts surrounding their termination and execution of the release. Appellants claimed to have been told by certain individuals in the Champlin organization that they had to sign and return the release by their termination date, less than 45 days after receiving the notice, in order to receive benefits under the Plan.

. . . .

DISCUSSION

Knowing and Voluntary Waiver

Congress, through enactment of the OWBPA, has determined that employers must afford their employees the right to consider for 45 days whether they should waive any rights or claims *vis á vis* the ADEA in exchange for benefits under a group termination program. 29 U.S.C. § 626(f)(1)(F)(ii). Appellants contend, *inter alia*, that Champlin denied them this right. Champlin responds by arguing that it complied with the 45-day requirement and pointing to the "Notice Pertaining to Release of Claims" document as proof. Appellants counter by swearing that the information contained therein was orally countermanded by certain persons at Champlin. Champlin, of course, denies that Appellants were told anything of the sort.

Which version accurately describes Champlin's dealings with Appellants is an issue that cannot be resolved by the court through summary judgment. . . . We are unable to conclude, therefore, that Appellants' releases were "knowing and voluntary" under the OWBPA. . . .

Exercise 3: Determining Substance

What should go into a contract for the sale of a house? An attorney-client retainer agreement? A statute dealing with stalking? Drafters frequently resort to commercial form books for checklists covering the substantive content of a particular type of private-law document or statutes in other jurisdictions for legislative drafting. A drafter, however, can custom-build a substantive checklist around the topics of **who** the document applies to, **what** conduct the document regulates, **when** the various acts are required or prohibited, **where** these acts must be performed or are prohibited from being performed, and **how** these acts are to be performed. *See* Haggard 64-77; Child 288-94.

This exercise involves the exploration of those five fundamental questions within two different private-law contexts.

1. A client that owns a small industrial company wants to hire a new office manager and needs an employment contract. You are to meet with her tomorrow to discuss the matter. Prepare a substantive checklist.

2. Your client has recently purchased a small apartment complex (10 apartments) near the University. It is currently being renovated but will be ready for occupancy soon. He has asked you to prepare a lease agreement that he can use. It will be a form agreement, with blank spaces for the tenant's name, the apartment number, and the dates. Prepare a substantive checklist.

Exercise 4: Testing for Substantive Gaps

Even the most careful drafter will sometimes create a document, in its initial versions at least, that contains *if...then* ambiguities (if X is satisfied, does this lead us to Y or Z?) and *blind alleys* (the satisfaction or non-satisfaction of X leads nowhere). The best way for identifying these drafting defects is by creating a flowchart of the document. With a flowchart and a real or hypothetical set of facts, one should be able to track through the statute, answer a series of *yes* or *no* questions relating to these facts, and arrive at a legal conclusion. If one cannot do that with a particular statute, then it is badly drafted. *See* Haggard 77-81.

1. A state legislator has drafted the following provision as an amendment to the tax code.

RIGHT TO REVIEW

> To obtain an administrative hearing of a Commission tax ruling, a person who has filed under section 12(b) or section 115 unless the tax-deferred credit exception applies must notify the Director of intent to appeal, provide documentation of the claim within 15 days thereafter, and if so requested in writing by the Director or by order of the administrative law judge assigned to hear the case sign a release for all bank records; to obtain direct review by the Director, such person must in addition place one-half of the contested amount in an escrow fund.

a. Prepare a flowchart of that provision.

b. After resolving any ambiguities in the statute, revise it to make it clearer.

2. You are staff counsel to the Senate Agriculture Committee. A member of the committee has drafted a bill dealing with the classification of agricultural land. He has asked you to review it for substantive gaps and ambiguities -- and, if you think appropriate, to redraft it. The material in brackets is not part of the statute.

Section 10-23-39.

(a) This section applies only to land that is outside the boundaries of a city incorporated pursuant to Section 7-17-37. [Assume that under state law "cities" are not the only legally recognized form of municipal government and that cities may be incorporated under several sections.]

(b) If such land is more than one mile outside the boundaries of any such city, is used for raising cattle or sheep in herds of 100 or more, has been so used for more than five years, and is also used as the principal residence of the owner or a tenant, it shall be classified as Agricultural Use A.

(c) If such land satisfies the requirements of subsection (b), above, but is not used as the principal residence of the owner or a tenant, it shall be classified as Agricultural Use B, unless the county in which said land exists has zoned the land for non-residential use only, in which case it shall be classified as Agricultural Use C.

(d) All other such land shall be classified as Agricultural Use D; provided, however, that the Secretary of Agriculture may designate such land for Agricultural Use E after notice to the landowner and an opportunity for a hearing.

a. Prepare a flowchart of that provision.

b. After resolving any ambiguities in the statute, revise it to make it clearer.

Exercise 5: Using Existing Legal Concepts in Drafting

Legal concepts are like off-the-rack clothing. They often provide a perfectly adequate way of expressing and implementing the client's objectives. The trick is to find the one that fits. *See* Haggard 82-85, 95-96.

Use a legal dictionary or *Words and Phrases* to answer these questions:

1. Senator Lawrence Arthur Wentworth, who is in his dotage and is getting forgetful, recently went into the Capital City Cafe, carefully hung his umbrella on the coat rack, ate a hearty breakfast, and then left -- leaving the umbrella on the coat rack. He visited the newsstand, the barber shop, and the bank. He roamed around the Capital Building for a while, and then went to his office. Later in the day, as he was about to leave the Capital, it started to rain. The Senator looked around his office for his umbrella, but was unable to locate it. He figured he had left it somewhere in his morning travels, but he could not remember where. He was very disturbed, because his late wife had given the umbrella to him. *Senator L.A.W.* was engraved on the handle.

Around mid-morning of that same day, William "Slick Willie" Malone had been in the Capital City Cafe. He was the only patron at the time. As he paid his bill, he noticed the umbrella on the coat rack. Since no one else was in the Cafe, he figured he could just take it. When he took it down from the coat rack, the owner of the Cafe objected, but Willie said "Losers weepers, finders keepers" and ran out of the Cafe. Willie noticed the engraving, but made no effort to locate the owner.

A week later, the Senator saw Willie with the umbrella and had him arrested for theft. The District Attorney, however, refused to prosecute, saying that Willie's conduct did not exactly fit under any of the existing criminal statutes.

You work in the Capital's Legislative Drafting Service. At the Senator's request, a bill has been drafted. In essence, it says that in a situation like that described above, the owner of the premises has the sole right to retain possession of the property pending a search for the true owner and that anyone else who takes the property is guilty of theft.

What is the most appropriate property law term/concept to use when creating a criminal statute dealing with the possession of property under the described circumstances -- *Abandoned Property*, *Lost Property*, or *Mislaid Property*?

2. The State Liquor Commission is required to hold hearings on all applications for a liquor license. The old statute allowed anyone who might be "adversely affected" by the grant or denial of a license to intervene. The facts in these matters are rarely in dispute. The question is always whether under the undisputed facts the "adversely affected" standard was satisfied. The Commission had adopted an extraordinarily narrow approach to the question of who was "adversely affected," while the courts in the state had adopted an extremely expansive definition. The result was a lot of unnecessary litigation.

The House Health & Welfare Committee has proposed an amendment that lists the criteria the Commission should consider in deciding whether to allow someone to intervene in a hearing. The Committee, however, wants to curtail judicial "second guessing" of the

Commission's decisions. As Representative Sarah Repeal puts it, "The Commission decision should stand unless it is arbitrary, capricious, unfair, or totally inconsistent with the facts and relevant criteria."

You have been asked to draft the provision dealing with judicial review of the Commission's decisions. Which standard of judicial review would best match Representative Repeal's description: *substantial evidence, clearly erroneous, preponderance of the evidence, abuse of discretion, clear and convincing evidence,* or *beyond a reasonable doubt*?

Exercise 6: Creating Suitable Factual Concepts

Creating factual concepts is an obtuse and slightly metaphysical process. Basically, it involves choices between the general versus the specific, the vague versus the precise, and the concrete versus the abstract. *See* Haggard 85-95; Child 303-13.

1. Think of some kind of problem (the *evil* to be corrected) that might arise in a University context. Start with Student X (a 2nd year law student who sits on the second row in this drafting class and is Professor Kingsfield's University-paid research assistant) as the most specific object of proposed regulation. Then expand the classifications (generalities) until you reach the broadest category that encompasses both Student X and addresses the evil to be corrected.

2. Assume the following levels of generality:

I. Employers
- A. Public employers [subdivisions as below]
- B. Private employers
  - 1. Less than 15 employees [subdivisions as below]
  - 2. 15-100 employees [subdivisions as below]
  - 3. 101 and more employees
    - a. Engaged in manufacturing [subdivisions as below]
    - b. Engaged in transportation
      - (1) Air transportation [subdivisions as below]
      - (2) Land transportation
        - (a) Carrying passengers only [subdivisions as below]
        - (b) Carrying goods only
          - (i) Intra-state [subdivisions as below]
          - (ii) Interstate

[A] Carrying non-toxic materials
[B] Carrying toxic materials
[1] Carrying non-radioactive materials
[2]Carrying radioactive materials

What would be the proper level of generality or the *operative concept* if the client's objective was:

a. To enact a regulation requiring drivers working for large trucking companies to wear radioactive monitoring badges?

b. To enact a statute making terminations in violation of the 5th or 14th Amendments an actionable tort?

c. To provide an exemption from certain tax rules for operators of small commercial planes?

3. What appears to be the lowest common denominator or the *operative concept* linking each of the following sets of entities? What would be an appropriate term to describe that concept?

a. Larry who is in law school; Mary who is in medical school; Victoria who is in veterinary school; and Donna who is in dental school.

Would Martin Luther, who is enrolled in Theology School, be a similar entity? What about Terry Turner, who is enrolled at Bevo Technical Colleges, studying Technical Writing?

b. The book *The Red Badge of Courage*, the movie *Hunt For Red October*, the comic strip *Beetle Bailey*, and a "Joe Camel [dressed in Army fatigues] Supports Desert Storm" billboard advertisement.

What if you add an audiotape of the book *General Custer at Little Big Horn* to the list?

c. A Ford Ranger pickup truck, a Mack Truck gravel hauler, a Norfolk Southern coal car, and a Mississippi River garbage barge.

What if you add a riding lawn mower? What if a double-decker bus manufactured in England is specifically excluded? What if an electric golf cart is also specifically excluded?

4. Provide a precise substitute for the following vague terms (use a legal dictionary or *Words and Phrases* if necessary):

a. within a reasonable time

b. necessaries (in relation to what a non-custodial parent must provide for his or her children)

c. net profits

d. fixtures

e. regular (in relation to when maintenance must be done on a machine)

f. serious misconduct (in relation to grounds for termination from employment)

g. clean and neat condition (in relation to a furnished apartment that is being rented)

h. intoxicated

5. Provide a vague term to replace the following precise terms:

a. within 24 hours after actual receipt of the notice of defect (in regard to when repair or replacement must occur)

b. assault and battery with intent to kill, attempted murder, bribery of a public official, carnal knowledge of a female child, perjury, soliciting for prostitution, embezzlement, extortion, fraudulent conversion, and larceny (in regard to the types of crimes for which a lawyer can be permanently disbarred)

c. 20 feet, plus or minus 3.5 inches (in regard to how close to the property line a home owner wants the nursery to plant a line of trees)

d. a personal contact if the person is in town; a certified letter if the person is out of town; a newspaper advertisement if the location of the person is unknown (regarding the efforts a creditor must make to contact the debtor before filing a lien on the property)

e. defects that will cost less than $2.00 to correct or repair (regarding what is not grounds for revoking acceptance of the goods)

Exercise 7: Organization

Drafted documents often contain a vast amount of complicated data. Organizing that data into something coherent uses the classical tools of division, classification, and sequence. *See* Haggard 97-104; Child 131-34, 199-02.

1. List the possible divisional criteria the following could be subject to:

6 b 8 **t** 13 # 12 **r** v s **5**

o **2** W ≥ c y s k **x** **q** 3

x B **j** j & 7 p 9 u u 8

2. Assume that you have tentatively decided to organize (divide) an apartment lease into the following categories:

A. The Parties
B. Description of Leased Premises
C. Security Deposit
D. Rent
E. Duration
F. Landlord's Rights and Duties
G. Tenant's Rights and Duties
H. Termination
I. Miscellaneous

Into which category would you then place the following bits of information (only a partial list of what might ultimately go into the lease):

a. At the termination of the lease, the Landlord may withhold from the security deposit any money owed for back rent, for damage to the apartment, or for other losses caused by Tenant's breach of the lease.

b. A *no oral modification* clause.

c. The Landlord is Cornell Apartments.

d. The Landlord is entitled to and the Tenant is obligated to allow the Landlord to enter the apartment to perform routine maintenance, to show the apartment to other prospective tenants during the last month of the lease, and to inspect for damage prior to Tenant's departure from the premises.

e. Except in cases of emergency, the Landlord will give and the Tenant is entitled to have at least 24 hours advance notice prior to the Landlord's entry into the apartment to perform routine maintenance, to show the apartment to other prospective tenants, or to inspect for damage.

f. The common areas that all Tenants may use include the parking lot, the volleyball court, the tennis court, the swimming pool, and clubhouse, and the washer/dryer room.

g. Rent is due on or before the first day of the month.

h. At the end of the initial term of the lease, the lease will automatically renew on a month-to-month basis unless either party gives at least one month's notice of intent to terminate the lease or unless the lease automatically terminates because of nonpayment of rent or other substantial breach of the lease terms.

3. Assume that you have drafted a set of Law School Honor Code Regulations, consisting of the following provisions. In what order would you arrange these provisions? Why? What subheadings would be appropriate?

a. Appeal from Honor Council decision to the Faculty.
b. Sanctions.
c. Student duty to report violations (with failure itself being an Honor Code violation).
d. Composition of Honor Council.
e. Definition of the prohibited classes of conduct.
f. Accused's right to written notice of charge.
g. Report of alleged violation to the Dean.
h. Time and place of hearing before Honor Council.
i. The Dean's investigation of alleged violation.
j. Statement of why an Honor Code is important in a law school.
k. Disposition of matter by the Dean on admission of guilt.
l. Accused's right to submit evidence to the Dean during the Dean's investigation of the charge.
m. The Dean's submission of unresolved charge to Honor Council.
n. Effective date.
o. Miscellaneous procedural matters relating to the hearing before Honor Council.
p. Appeal from the Faculty to the University Disciplinary Committee.
q. Authority of Honor Council to enforce Honor Code.
r. Accused student's right to confront accusers, to cross examine witnesses, to introduce evidence, and to be represented by counsel.
s. Violation of Honor Code is based on a preponderance of the evidence standard.
t. Responsibility of the Student Prosecutor.
u. Dismissal of charge by the Dean.

v. Report of Honor Council.

Exercise 8: Avoiding Ambiguities

Ambiguity is the *summum malum* of drafting -- the ultimate evil to be avoided. Three kinds of ambiguity exist: contextual ambiguity, semantic ambiguity, and syntactical ambiguity. *See* Haggard 105-52; Child 315-42.

Identify and cure (as your discretion dictates) all the ambiguities in the following hypothetical provisions. Read them from the perspective of the *reader in bad faith* -- namely, a person who will exploit every possible loophole to gain even the slightest advantage, even if it is nothing more than a litigation settlement chit. Thus, do not let common sense blind you to the arguments that this person might make -- arguments that may well fail, but only after expensive litigation. Some of the examples may contain multiple ambiguities.

a. The *Bluebook*, Rule 12.9 at page 87:

> Note that except when referring to the U.S. Code provisions, the word "section" should be spelled out in law review text and footnote text, although the symbol "§" may be used in citations. See **rule 6.2(b).**

The *Bluebook*, Rule 6.2(b) at page 49:

> [S]pell out the words "section" and "paragraph" in the text (whether main text or footnote text) of law review pieces and other documents, except when

referring to a provision in the U.S. Code, a state code, or a federal regulation (see **rule 12.9**).

b. The Chair and Vice Chair may nominate up to three candidates for admission.

c. This prohibition applies to papers written by students and faculty.

d. Students in Legal Writing § 1 and Torts § 3 must attend the Wednesday orientation session.

e. The winner will be a student chosen from Professor Hamilton's and Professor Wright's sections.

f. Students on Law Review, possessing a 3.4 average, and certified by the Associate Dean are entitled to apply for the exception.

g. For this weekend only, employees may apply to work overtime on Saturday or Sunday. Because only a limited number of positions are available, for each of these days the work will be awarded to employees on the basis of seniority.

h. With respect to all packaged meat products entering the facility, the delivery dock inspector must certify that the USDA seal was intact at the time of delivery or the Head Cook may conduct bacterial tests, which must be paid for by seller.

i. To graduate, a student must take either Advanced Commercial Law (4 credits) or Sales (2 credits) and Commercial Paper (2 credits).

j. To graduate, a student must take Drafting and/or Real Estate Transactions.

k. A zoning variance may be obtained upon: (a) proof of a varying use prior to June 1, 1996; (b) proof that the public interest will be served by the variance; (c) written consent of adjoining property owners.

l. To be eligible for the severance package, an employee who is being terminated must sign the ADEA waiver form between October 1, 2000, and October 15, 2000.

m. If a law school applicant has not filed a notice of intent to matriculate by June 1, 2002, that student's acceptance will be automatically revoked.

n. An applicant for public assistance during the 2000-01 fiscal year has until July 1, 2000, to provide proof of indigency.

o. Subject to the termination-by-notice provision of this contract, Buyer's obligation to purchase all its Carbolic Smoke Balls from Seller continues until the end of the 20th Century.

p. A terminated employee has until 14 days after the time the notice of termination is given to file a grievance.

q. Measured from the day on which the notice of termination is given, an employee may transfer into another department without penalty before the 20th day; an employee may transfer into another department with loss of seniority after the 20th day and before the 30th day; an employee has no transfer rights after the 30th day.

r. [Offer dated July 1, 2000] You must accept this offer within 14 days.

s. [Notice of intent to terminate credit account, dated Wednesday, July 10, 2000] To avoid a $100 penalty, you must at least pay the accrued interest within 5 days.

t. Landlord agrees to clean the pool bimonthly and have a Department of Health bacteria inspection semiannually.

u. This contest begins at midnight on October 1, 2000, and ends at noon on October 31, 2000.

v. [Order of the Zoning Commission dated July 28, 1997] Whenever the Zoning Commissioner contemplates a change in the zoning category of a piece of residential property, it shall send by registered mail a notice of the proposed change to all persons presently residing within 12 blocks of that property.

w. All persons over the age of 15 must pay full adult fare.

x. Buyer will accept delivery on October 31, 2000, provided, however, that prior to that time Seller provides proof of clear title.

y. 1. Job categories are divided into three groups:

(a) Group # 1: Captain, First Mate, First Engineer, and Cook.

(b) Group # 2: Second Engineer, Assistant Cook, Crew, Net Handlers, and Dock Handlers. All the job categories referenced hereinabove are also subject to Section 6(b) of the Union contract.

(c) Group # 3: Apprentice Seamen, longshoremen, and temporary employees in all categories.

z. The 12 football tickets will be divided between the Dean and members of the Faculty.

aa. Contractor will install a loading dock with a sloped ramp on the side and it will be 18 feet long.

bb. Employees on the second shift will be assigned some of the duties formerly performed by employees on the first shift, and such employees will be entitled to bid for jobs on the carbolic production line.

cc. This leave policy applies to pregnant production department employees, shipping department employees, and R&D employees who have not otherwise exhausted their optional leave time.

dd. This section applies to motorized vehicles, except those used in connection with the business and not licensed for road use.

ee. Every employee with a spouse working in the Longtown Plant is entitled to participate in the Plan.

ff. If damaged during shipment between Boston and New York, the standard rail car on which the goods were loaded at Boston will be replaced with a Conrail Supershock rail car for further shipment to Washington, D.C.

gg. Only persons who were employed within two weeks prior to the effective date of the policy are required to provide the supplemental information listed below.

hh. Every spouse of an employee with dependents of a prior marriage may opt for full coverage.

ii. Seller will provide the lumber, pipes, and insulating material, but is not required to deliver the lumber to Buyer's work site.

jj. If Buyer does not specifically request delivery by rail, Seller is not obligated to ship by that method. [Buyer does request delivery by rail. Is Seller obligated?]

kk. If Seller is to be obligated to ship by rail, then Buyer must request it. [Buyer does request shipment by rail. Is Seller obligated?]

ll. Dogs may be prohibited from the premises because of tendencies for barking.

mm. Employees with less than 10 years seniority are not eligible to hold 1st shift jobs unless the shift supervisor consents in writing. No employee with less than 4 hours of OSHA disaster response training is eligible for 1st shift jobs.

nn. Subcontractors only are subject to sections 45(a)-(t).

oo. Owner and contractor agree that authorization by the City Building Code Commissioner will be obtained and the $1,000 fee paid before construction begins.

pp. All students must take an advanced legal writing course which includes legal drafting.

qq. Applicants for pre-school tuition aid must being their children to the Department of Social Services for an interview.

rr. An employee who completes the February training session will receive a $10 bonus and a certificate signed by the Plant Manager.

ss. Every student must write a five-page paper on each of the following: Moses, the founding of modern Israel, Jesus and the right to die.

tt. The prohibition against carrying weapons in vehicles on company property does not apply to the vehicles of employees on the first shift

(11:00 p.m. to 6:00 a.m.) who park in Lot A; nor does it apply to the storage of weapons in the trunk of a car if that car is parked in lots B, C, or D.

Exercise 9: Drafting Style and Usage

Simplicity, clarity, and brevity are the benchmarks of all good legal writing. Drafted documents simply take these principles of composition to the ultimate. *See* Haggard 153-203; Child 375-407.

Identify what is stylistically wrong with and edit the following provisions. More than one thing may be wrong with several of them.

a. Cleanup, Inc., will sell, subject to the following terms, industrial solvent to the Needsitmucho Company: . . . . Seller warrants that . . . . but buyer agrees to use the solvent only . . . . Supplier further warrants that . . . , subject to user's compliance with EPA Regulation 445-8-c-(33)q.

b. Contractor will: (a) install a lawn sprinkling system; (b) allowing the system to be tested and approved by a certified IQEW inspector; (c) restoration of disturbed sod; and (d) signs warning persons when the system will come on automatically.

c. A. This section is intended to provide preliminary information about the parties, the coverage of the contract, and other general matters that will assist in the interpretation of this contract.

1. Parties. The parties to this contract are Cleanup, Inc., and the Needsitmucho Company.

2. Site Covered. The chemical cleanants covered by the terms of this contract will be used exclusively at the Needsitmucho Company's commercial laundry facility located at 666 Danger Road, Cesspool, Yourstate, 46321.

. . . .

R. CHEMICALS/COMPOUNDS NOT COVERED: The following chemicals and chemical compounds are not covered by this contract:

(a) Dimerriamwebsterchronocyclamate.
(b) Collegiatedictionarious-hydrogenated.
(c) Fiberfaced-pollygrinus secretions.

. . . .

W. Exceptions -- The provisions of this contract do not apply to:

§ W.1 -- Any cleaning that is conducted in connection with laundry from the U.S. Navy Nuclear Testing Facility at Port Kall.

. . . .

§ W.13: Any cleaning that is conducted in connection with laundry certified as Class B by the State Health Department.

d. Manager is an at-will employee and Company may terminate Manager at any time and for any reason or no reason at all. Manager is an at-will employee and may resign at any time and for any reason or no reason at all. As an at-will employee, Manager has no right to be terminated only "for cause."

e. Whereas, in consideration and exchange for $10,000 and other good and sufficient consideration, the aforementioned being over, above, and in addition to whatever compensation, pay, or consideration is otherwise hereinbefore or hereinafter due and owing to John Jones (hereinafter referred to as "Manager") in connection with the termination, end, and cessation of his employment, in hand paid, said Manager agrees, covenants, and contracts to provide a full and complete release and discharge of the Sundial Company (hereinafter referred to as "Company") for each, all, and every claim, charge, and cause of action of every kind and nature arising out of or relating to Manager's employment. Any, all, and every contract[s], covenant[s], agreement[s] or understanding[s] between Manager and Company that are to the contrary or inconsistent with, or contradict, the terms, provisions, conditions, and promises contained herein are null, void, and of no force and effect.

Manager further agrees that all private, secret, and confidential papers in Manager's possession will be returned to Company or completely destroyed, that for the period of time of one year Manager will not be employed by any competitor of Company located within a distance of 100 miles of said Company's facility, located in the City of Columbia, County of Richland, State of South Carolina, United States of America.

f. In order to file a claim with respect to injuries that have occurred in the course of the work day, an employee must have medical costs that are in excess of $100. In the event that the employee claims the injuries will cause a permanent disability with the result that the employee can no longer work, the claim will be held in abeyance until such time as this can be determined.

g. Buyer will pay $10,000 for the goods. Next, Buyer will accept delivery of the goods at the Galveston rail terminal, although Seller will provide at least 10 days notice of the delivery date. In addition, Seller will obtain for the Buyer a pass into the terminal. On the other hand, Buyer will use a bonded common carrier to transport the goods from the terminal to the Buyer's facility.

h. This subsection applies to all of the dependents of an applicant who are listed in section 3(a). An applicant who is submitting documentary evidence of dependency must comply with the Guidelines of the Commissioner, which were promulgated on June 3, 1996. The documents that an applicant submits must be verified. Applicants have twenty (20) days to complete the file.

i. Section 1. It is the public policy of the State of California to promote a pollution-free environment. Public policy, however, also gives recognition to the need for a healthy economy. It is the purpose of this Act to provide an accommodation for those two goals.

. . . .

Section 7. There are 10 factors that the Department of Health and Environmental Control shall give consideration to when deciding whether to grant approval of a wetlands dredging operation.

j. An application for a visa extension must be filed by a resident alien on or before June 1, 2000. An extension may be granted if the work area has been certified as Class 4 by the Department of Labor.

k. If the parties are in agreement, the contractor is under an obligation to then proceed with installation. If the parties are unable to agree, the dispute is to be submitted to an arbitration that is binding.

l. After Owner and Contractor have agreed on a construction schedule, they will, unless the Surety requires it earlier, file that schedule by no later than 10 days before construction begins, and they will periodically update the schedule as construction proceeds, to reflect delays as they occur.

m. If inclement weather caused a delay, the contractor's duty will be excused. But if the contractor could have avoided the delay by rescheduling the order in which work proceeds, then contractor had a duty to do that.

n. At the expiration of the comment period, the Director shall forthwith promulgate regulations requiring owners of properties contiguous to the site to procure hazardous waste insurance and to execute a release waiving all rights to remuneration for damage caused by the government.

o. (1) An employer who engages in a corporate employee-component reduction exercise must give the employees 30 days advance notice.

(2) Applicants may obtain their pre-existing medical condition disclosure forms from the Director of Health.

p. (1) The vehicle is not safe.

(2) The exception does not apply to persons with more than 3 children.

(3) Under Rule 36, a defendant who does not plead not guilty is not entitled to representation by the Public Defender.

q. All law students at the University of Texas, except those whose legal residence is in Texas, must complete Form 765-3.

r. (1) An applicant whose file has not been acted upon within 60 days is entitled to begin receiving benefits and he may also file a notice of noncompliance with the Commissioner.

(2) Unless a contractor complies with this provision, he will be personally liable for providing workers' compensation insurance.

(3) The Director of the Agency shall make the termination decision. If he decides to terminate, the decision is final.

(4) A member of the Supreme Court or the Court of Appeals must certify the appeal. He must then file a motion for self-disqualification.

(5) If a defendant does not assert his privilege against self-incrimination in a timely fashion, it will be considered waived.

(6) Section 3 applies to a dog that is over 100 pounds. If he is one of the breeds listed in Section 6, then Section 4 also applies.

(7) He who elects to proceed under Rule 6 must complete Form 334-9.

(8) [In an employment manual] Each employee must supply his own steel-toed shoes.

(9) [In a student handbook] A student must be punctual in getting to his 8:00 a.m. classes.

(10) Each applicant must provide his Social Security number.

(11) When a contractor subcontracts, he must notify the owner within 10 days.

(12) An employee must file his application for leave at least 10 days in advance.

Exercise 10: Creating Definitions

By giving a complex legal or factual concept a label, definitions promote clarity. By eliminating the need to repeat the full verbal formula of that concept every time it appears in a document, definitions also promote brevity. Definitions, however, are powerful medicine and are often needlessly and dangerously used. *See* Haggard 204-26; Child 355-74.

1. What is wrong with the following definitions?

   a. "Pencil" means an implement for writing, drawing, or marking consisting of or containing a slender cylinder or strip of solid marking substance surrounded by a wood, metal, or plastic sheath.

   b. "Pencil" includes a paint brush, a spray can, a ball point pen, a fountain pen, and a felt-tip marker.

   c. "Felony" means murder, assault with intent to kill, armed robbery, arson, kidnapping, rape, first degree sexual assault, lynching, child molestation, and other felonies.

   d. As used in these regulations, "new animal drug" means any form of medicine for animals that has been developed since January 1, 1996, except that the Secretary of Agriculture may exempt such drug from regulation if the Secretary finds that the drug is safe, effective, and pure.

e. "Tax exempt bonds" means and includes bonds issued under Section 347 of the Securities Act of 1937.

2. Create:

a. A full or stipulative definition for some areas that might be regarded as common areas (shared by all tenants) in a large apartment complex.

b. A full or stipulative definition for a class of entities consisting of cows, horses, mules, pigs, goats, sheep, and chickens.

c. An enlarging definition that will ensure that part-time students, transient students, and persons who are auditing a course are subject to a school rule that affects "students."

d. A limiting definition that ensures that teaching assistants, adjuncts, visiting professors, retired professors, and nonacademic deans are not subject to a rule that affects "faculty."

e. A limiting definition that ensures that a typewritten name does not satisfy the requirement for a "signed writing."

f. A full or stipulative definition that ensures that only a handwritten signature satisfies the requirement for a "signed writing."

Exercise 11: Creating Legal Consequences

The whole purpose of a drafted document, whether it is a private-law document or legislation, is to create certain legal consequences. These include rights, duties, privileges, conditions, and others. Various terminological conventions exist for creating these consequences. *See* Haggard 227-44; Child 204-07.

1. In a statute, create a duty for a person who has a swimming pool on the property to put a fence around it.

2. In a construction contract, create a duty for the builder to use Reading brand pipe.

3. In a city ordinance, create a duty on a police officer to not exceed the posted speed limit unless the blue light and siren are on.

4. In a partnership agreement, create a duty on each partner to not engage in any business that is in competition with the business of the partnership.

5. Assume that in a construction contract the builder can use substitute materials if the materials called for in the specifications are unavailable, but that it is also customary in the industry to inform the owner first. Draft a provision that excuses the contractor from that implied duty.

6. Assume that a landlord-tenant statute gives the tenant the right to assign the lease, unless the lease agreement provides otherwise.

Draft a lease provision that negates that statutory right.

7. Assume that a landlord-tenant statute makes the assignment of leases invalid, unless the lease agreement provides otherwise. Draft a lease provision that so provides.

8. In a government environmental regulation, draft a provision that requires regulated entities to file a Form 675-r application if they want to request permission to exceed established pollution discharge limits.

9. Assume that in a supply contract the seller has to provide all of the wingdings that the buyer needs, but the parties want to agree to suspend the seller from that obligation whenever the price of carbonmetalic compound goes over $1.50 per pound. Draft a provision to accomplish that.

10. Assume that in a construction contract the parties want to provide that the contractor has a duty to obtain the building inspector's approval of the foundations and only then will the owner have the duty to make the first partial payment. Draft a provision that accomplishes this.

11. The parties want the effective date of the contract to be July 4, 2002. Draft a provision that makes it so.

Exercise 12: The Rules of Interpretation

When confronted with a drafted document, a court will construe it according to the *rules of interpretation* that have evolved over the years. Although most of these rules are invoked only as a result of bad drafting -- which, if avoided, would render them superfluous -- the conscientious drafter nevertheless needs to draft with these rules in mind. *See* Haggard 245-66.

This exercise requires you to identify (1) the various rules of interpretation that a court might use, (2) what went wrong in the drafting process (thus making the use of these rules necessary), and (3) how this might have been avoided by more astute drafting.

1. A provision in the State Administrative Procedures Act reads as follows:

> A petition for review of final agency decisions must be filed in Circuit Court within 30 days after the decision is rendered.

Assume that on September 1 the State Department of Environmental Control rendered a written decision denying James Joyce's application to construct a marina on Waller Creek. A copy of the decision was mailed to Mr. Joyce, but it was erroneously sent to "4567 Ulysses Street" rather than to "7654 Ulysses Street," which was the address Mr. Joyce used on his application. The person residing at the first address was in London at the time the mail was delivered and did not return until mid-October. However, she immediately sent the envelope to Mr. Joyce at his correct address and he received it on October 16. Mr. Joyce filed his petition for review on October 18.

What argument can you make that Mr. Joyce's petition is untimely and should be dismissed? What argument can you make to the contrary? How could the problem have been avoided by better drafting?

2. Assume that in 1941 the state legislature enacted a statute providing an exception to the state Blue Laws, as follows:

> Notwithstanding Code § 356.1, it shall not be unlawful to exhibit publicly motion pictures, athletic sports and musical concerts and to engage therein from and after two p.m. on Sunday in counties wherein the United States Government has established and maintains permanent or temporary Army Forts, Naval or Marine bases.

The legislative history indicates that the statute was enacted at a time when the United States was inducting millions of individuals into the Armed Forces and providing almost around-the-clock training at facilities all over the county. Specifically, the legislature was aware that Sunday afternoon was the only time in which most members of the military were consistently free to engage in recreational activities. The statute was designed to allow them to engage in the activities listed.

The United States Government established an "Army Air Base" in Greenville County. Subsequently, the owner of the Majestic Theater in the City of Greenville was arrested for showing a movie on Sunday afternoon in violation of the Blue Laws.

What argument can you make that he should be convicted? What argument can you make that the exception applies? How could the drafters of this statute have avoided the problem?

3. A state job reference statute provides that an employer has an absolute privilege to provide certain types of information about former employees if the information is provided in writing.

George Jones, the Plant Manager at Acme Industrials, recently gave an oral job reference on Rae Bell Knight in which he stated that she had been suspended three times for being under the influence of drugs while at work. Jones had a reasonable, well-founded, and good faith belief that this was true. However, it was not true. Knight has sued Jones for defamation. Jones asserts his qualified common law privilege. Knight argues that the statute has superseded the common law rule. What argument can Jones make to the contrary? How could this problem have been avoided?

4. A federal statute bans the interstate shipment of any "obscene book, pamphlet, picture, motion-picture film, paper, letter, writing, print, or other matter of an indecent nature." The owner of Melody Records has been arrested for sending admittedly obscene phonograph records across state lincs. What argument can the owner make that phonograph records are not covered by the statute? What argument can the government make that they are? How could the statute have been drafted to avoid this problem?

5. A state statute imposes an ownership tax on every "rifle, shotgun, archery bow, punt boat, and all-terrain vehicle that is used for hunting within the State." The money is designated for use by the State Wildlife Agency.

Sam Colt owns the rifle that his father used in World War II. He keeps it on a wall with other memorabilia of that War. He has never shot it or used it for hunting, although ammunition is still available. The State Department of Revenue has assessed a tax on the rifle, with penalties. What argument will the State make the rifle is subject to the tax? What argument will Colt make that the rifle is not covered? How could the statute be revised to make it clear that this rifle is not covered?

6. Suppose the by-laws of a legal organization provide as follows:

> Law students and full-time faculty members may join the Law Student Division and Faculty Division by paying an additional $10 per year.

Willy Wiseacre, a third year law student, has applied to join the Faculty Division. What rule of construction will prevent him from doing this?

7. Susan Slick, representing Sam Seller, drafted a contract for the sale of goods between Seller and Bill Buyer. One provisions reads as follows:

> After delivery, if Buyer determines that the goods are defective within 20 days Seller must replace them.

Thirty days after the goods were delivered Buyer determined that the goods were defective. Seller, however, refuses to replace them, claiming that the determination was not made within the requisite 20 days. What argument can Buyer make to the contrary?

8. A state attachment statute provides for a priority lien on "motor vehicles" in favor of anyone "injured or damaged by the negligent or reckless operation thereof."

The object was to provide an *in rem* type of recovery. The statute does not define the phrase "motor vehicle." However, for the purposes of the state licensing and registration statute, the purpose of which is to enable an owner to establish title and to provide revenue to the state, the word "motor vehicle" is defined as "all vehicles independently propelled by gasoline, diesel, propane, any other explosive gas or liquid, steam, or electricity."

While Dave Dorset was driving his Mack Truck with an attached but detachable trailer, he carelessly turned a corner too quickly and swung the trailer into the car of Sarah Elizabeth, totally destroying her car and seriously injuring Sarah. Dave was given a ticket. He drove home, detached the trailer (which was only slightly damaged), got back into his Mack Truck and drove off -- never to be seen again. Draggah Trailer Company has a lien on the trailer. Sarah, however, has used the state attachment statute to impose a lien on the trailer that is superior to that of Draggah. Draggah argues that a trailer is not a "motor vehicle" and the attachment statute does not apply.

What rule of construction will Draggah rely on? What rule of construction will Sarah rely on? Who do you think should win?

9. A state unfair trade practices act defines unfair trade practices and provides for damages to parties injured by them and for certain kinds of equitable relief. However, the statute expressly provides that "a Master in Equity shall not have the power to issue a preliminary injunction, prior to a trial on the merits, for any practice proscribed by this act." In the past, a preliminary injunction against certain types of business practices operated as a *fiat accompli*; it would put a competitor out of business and by the time of the trial on the merits, the issue would be moot.

Freddy Fender Bender Towing Service solicits business in a manner that not only arguably violates the unfair trade practices act, but also probably constitutes common law fraud. One of the victims of this practice, Straight Arrow Towing, has sued for damages under the act and also for common law fraud. Straight Arrow has sought a preliminary injunction against the practice. Freddy argues that the act prohibits the issuance of a preliminary injunction.

What rule of statutory construction can Straight Arrow rely on? What if Freddy argues that the statute preempts the field and that a fraud cause of action no longer exists for this?

10. A state statute prohibits anyone from bringing a "weapon" onto any publicly owned sports stadium, coliseum, or other facility in which sporting events are conducted. Elizabeth Borden has been arrested under this statute for possessing an ice pick at the Gotham City high school football stadium.

What rule of statutory interpretation will she invoke to challenge her conviction under this statute?

11. A law school regulation provides as follows: "Students with sight impairments, hearing impairments, or mobility impairments that have been certified as such by the Office of Student Affairs are entitled to the following rights and privileges: . . ." Hank Lugoff is totally blind, but his impairment has never been "certified as such" by the appropriate office. Nevertheless, he claims he is entitled to the listed rights and privileges. What rule of interpretation might he rely on to support that claim?

Exercise 13: Drafting Ethics

The lawyer-drafter is subject to the same ethical rules that govern the entire profession. What these rules mean in the context of drafting is not, however, always crystal clear. *See* Haggard 323-52.

As your firm's resident expert in legal ethics, you are frequently asked to advise other members of the firm on various ethical issues. What advice would you give in the following situations? Why?

1. Attorney Anne has been contacted by an author (a non-lawyer) who is writing a do-it-yourself law book designed for a lay audience. He has asked her to draft some "simple," fill-in-the-blanks contracts -- sale of a house, loan agreement, contract for services, sales agreement, and the like. He also wants to list her as a contributor and as a "widely recognized specialist in legal drafting."

2. Attorney Bill has drafted lease agreement forms for the owners of several large apartment complexes and many individual landlords. None are considered currently active clients. The legislature recently enacted some legislation that makes several provisions in these leases illegal. A landlord who attempted to enforce them would be subject to a fairly substantial civil penalty in a suit brought by a tenant.

Bill wants to write all of these former clients a letter informing them of the change in the law and suggesting that their lease agreements be revised. In addition, since the firm is currently trying to encourage clients who are using the firm for one purpose (real estate transactions, for example) to also use the firm for other purposes (employment litigation, for example), Bill wants to include a paragraph that describes, in glowing terms, the firm's other areas of practice.

3. Attorney Charlie, who has just graduated from law school, tells you over lunch one day that his uncle, who is in the construction business, wants Charlie to draft a contract for the construction of a large shopping center, where the uncle's compensation will be in the form of a share of the ownership of the property rather than in cash, but with the other owners having an option to buy him out at the end of ten years. The uncle thinks he will incur substantial tax savings by doing it this way.

You ask Charlie if he is familiar with the construction business. He says "no," but that he figures he can find a construction contract in a form book. You ask him if he has looked into the tax angle. He says "no," but that his uncle said not to worry about that because his uncle was pretty sure it was legal. Charlie thinks this is a wonderful opportunity for him to make a name for himself in the firm. What do you think?

4. Attorney Danielle has been asked to draft a lease agreement containing some provisions that she knows will be void and unenforceable under the state landlord-tenant act -- a provision, for example, in which the tenant agrees not to allow children to reside on the premises. She says she told the client that these provisions could not be enforced, but the client wants them in the lease anyway (believing that the tenants will comply with them, unaware of the unenforceability).

5. Attorney Edgar is drafting a contract for his client involving the sale of several parcels of land within a large subdivision/condominium and golf complex that the client is developing. The client has agreed to sell and the buyer agreed to buy 103 separate parcels, but they cannot agree

on some parcels that are located in one corner of the development, consisting partially of a parcel known locally as the Wilson tract and another known as the Woodrow tract. The parcels in question are shown below:

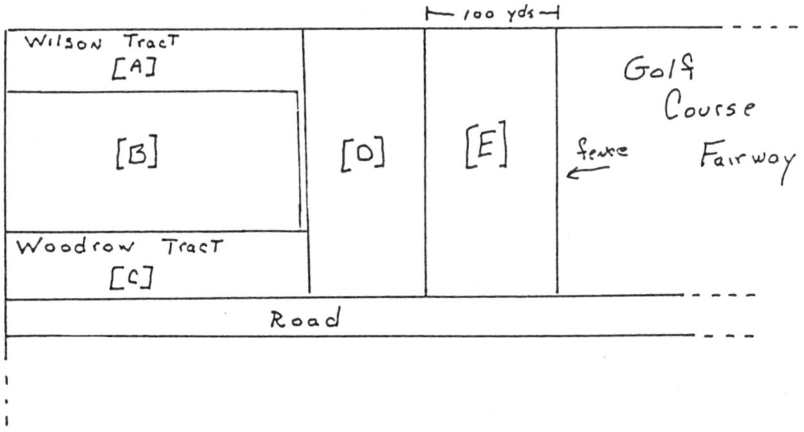

For convenience sake, Edgar and the client refer to the parcels by reference to the bracketed letters. The narrow, six-inch wide strip that is part of the Wilson tract is a result of sloppy surveying when the land was originally subdivided. Without seeing a plat, one would not even know it was part of the Wilson tract.

The client is willing to sell parcel D but wants to retain the other parcels for subdivision use. The buyer, however, is not interested in parcel D, but insists upon having the land contained in parcels B and E and may back out of the whole deal unless he gets them. Edgar has proposed to draft a provision identifying the land to be sold as "that land situated between the Wilson tract and the Woodrow tract and the tract extending in a westerly direction 100 yards from the fence at the end of the golf course fairway."

You question his strategy and he explains: "When the buyer reads that, he will think my client has given in to his demand and that he is getting the land between the Wilson tract and the Woodrow tract, what we call parcel B, and all of what we call parcel E. So, he will sign the contract. But when we actually draw up a plat and convey title, we will convey only parcel D, which lies between the combined parcels A/C, on one side, and parcel E, on the other. One of three things will happen, two of them good: First, the seller may simply accept our interpretation of the contract. Second, the seller may litigate but the court will adopt our interpretation of the contract. Third, the seller may litigate and the court will accept his interpretation of the contract -- in which case we will, of course, sell him parcels B and E. But we win in two out of three of the scenarios. Pretty clever, eh?"

6. Attorney Francis drafted a complex franchise agreement that her client, Texas Tom's Tacos, Inc., uses with all its franchisees. It took her thirty hours, which she billed at $85 an hour. Several months later, she sent the same document (with only names and minor details being changed) to Caroline's Bar-B-Q, Inc., for use with its franchisees. She also billed this client for 30 hours at $85 and hour. Caroline's legal department thought the bill was excessive and protested to your firm's Managing Partner, who sent it to you for review. You discover that Francis actually only spent 45 minutes reviewing Texas Tom's franchise agreement and revising it slightly for Caroline's use. What should the firm do?

7. Attorney George, who is Of Counsel to the firm, is the retired CEO of a major textile company. Until he joined the firm, he had never actively practiced law. Even now, he operates mainly as a *rain maker* for the firm, using his extensive business contacts to bring in legal work for the other attorneys in the firm.

Several months ago, he was consulted by his friend Sam Rayon, Vice President of Pine Tree Fabrics, concerning a proposed merger between Pine Tree and Wateree River Textiles. George was sent a copy of the proposed merger agreement and asked to review its terms. He did so and was concerned over a provision under which Pine Tree would be obligated to sell its shares in a wholly owned subsidiary, Finch Thread and Needle Company. To better understand how this sale would impact on the merged company, with Rayon's consent George called Carol Swanson, Director of Sales with Finch, and asked for certain information about market shares, Finch's expansion plans, and other information. Swanson sent him the information in writing. Reassured that the sale would not impact negatively on the new company and that indeed it was a very wise thing to do (Finch was in serious difficulty), George told Rayon that he thought they ought to go ahead with the merger, since "it makes good business sense." The merger was accomplished and Finch was sold Carlton Canvas, Inc.

Several months later, Carlton Canvas brought a conspiracy to defraud action against Rayon and other officers of the two corporations. George has been served with a subpoena for all documents in his possession involving the sale of Finch Thread and Needle Company. The information he receiving from Swanson, when viewed in light of certain other facts, strongly implicates the defendants. George does not want to provide the data. He has come to you for advice.

8. The firm publishes something it calls a *Client News Letter* and a *Client Alert*, containing general information about legal matters, reports about recent case decisions, simple articles on how to avoid legal difficulty, and the like. The mailing list for the *Letter* and *Alert* contains virtually anyone the firm has ever represented, plus

various public officials, trade associations, and law professors.

Ten years ago attorney Hannah drafted a franchise agreement that New York Hot Dogs, Inc., has used with all its franchisees. New York Hot Dogs is the largest hot dog chain in the country, with thousands of franchises. The franchise agreement that Hannah drafted heavily favors the corporation over the franchise owners. Neither she nor anyone else in the firm has represented New York Hot Dogs since then, but the company is on the mailing list of the *Letter* and *Alert*.

Recently, the franchise owners formed the NYHD Franchise Owner's Association. They have asked Hannah to draft a franchise agreement on their behalf that will be more favorable to them than the current one is and to represent them in negotiations with New York Hot Dogs.

New York Hot Dogs has found out about this and is protesting Hannah's involvement.

PART II

Exercise 14: An Overview

You recently received the following letter from your old college roommate, Charles Black:

Dear Roomie,

I hope things are going well with you and the practice of law. I continue to enjoy working for Metropolitan Life. I may drive up to Charleston to visit you when the family gathers at Edisto Beach at Thanksgiving.

Frankly, I am not looking forward to it -- again! Specifically, the mandatory touch football game. As you know, tradition requires that I do the kickoffs. Tradition also requires that my cousin Lucinda hold the football for me. Unfortunately, **she** thinks tradition also requires that she pull the ball away (at least on the initial kickoff and sometimes also during the game) -- causing me to fall on my butt, to the great hilarity of the rest of the family.

I have asked her to stop, but she just laughs at me and once said, "So sue me, already." Right! Lucinda has a law firm on full time retainer and thinks litigation is the great American indoor sport. And with the money she inherited from Harry after he died three years ago, she can afford it.

Last year, she actually promised not to

pull the ball away on purpose. She did anyway, and claimed she had a muscle spasm. And, she said, "An oral promise is as good as the paper it is written on."

Anyway, I will give you a call and perhaps we can get together.

Your friend,
Charlie
Charlie

What a sad story. Think about it from a drafter's perspective.

Exercise 15: Surety Agreement

Background: On a construction job, the contract between the owner and the contractor/builder usually requires the contractor/builder to post a surety or performance bond. This bond is in the form of a contract between the contractor/builder and the surety (usually an insurance company). The contractor/builder is referred to as the "Principal" and the owner is referred to as the "Obligee" (since this is who the surety company owes the obligation to, as a third party beneficiary of the contract).

This particular provision of the typical surety agreement is intended to describe the circumstances under which the obligation of the surety company terminates. It reads as follows:

> Now, THEREFORE, the condition of this obligation [the surety's obligation to pay the Obligee] is such that if the Principal shall faithfully perform the work on his part to be performed, and shall fully indemnify and save harmless the Obligee from all claims and demands incurred by the Principal in the performance of said contract [the construction contract between the owner/Obligee and the builder/contractor/Principal]; and from all loss or damage which may arise to the Obligee by reason of any default on the part of the Principal, then this obligation shall be null and void; otherwise it shall remain in full force and effect.

a. Be prepared to critique this provision in class. Look for excessive wordiness, lack of clarity, potential ambiguities, defective grammar and punctuation, and the like.

b. Try to figure out what this provision is really trying to say. Once you have done so, then draft a simplified version of it. However, retain the basic approach by identifying the circumstances under which the surety's obligation is discharged.

Exercise 16: Contract For the Sale of a Car

Sally Celler and Bill Beyer have asked you to draft a contract for them. Celler owns a 1948 two-door, black Chevrolet, VIN5-6670p2vvfkd76709. It has special South Carolina "classic car" license plates, TRH 1939. Celler has agreed to sell it to Beyer for $4,000. Beyer will give her a $1,000 down payment and then $150 a month for the next 20 months. The tags will be assigned with the car. Beyer will pay the fee to transfer title and tags. Celler will retain a lien on the car until the car is paid for.

The old '48 Chevy had something called a "vacuum shift." It was supposed to make shifting easier, but it frequently did not work and caused other transmission problems. For example, the second gear on this car does not work and Celler has advised Beyer of this. Celler, however, thinks everything else is fine but she does not to warrant anything about the condition of the car. [See UCC 2-316.]

Beyer also knows that Mike Mecanichek worked on the car recently. Celler says that Mecanichek has been paid in full for his work, but Beyer wants Sally to warrant the car is being delivered free of any rightful claims (mechanic's or other liens) by Mecanichek or other third parties and that she has good title herself. She has agreed to do this. [This would be an implied warranty if Celler were a merchant, which she is not. See UCC 2-312).

Beyer will take delivery of the car when he pays the down payment, at Celler's home, 647 Rivershore Drive, Longtown, South Carolina. They have agreed that the sale will take place two weeks from the date of the contract. During this time, however, Bill wants to be able to take the car to a mechanic of his choice and to rescind the contract if the mechanical condition of the car is found not to be to Beyer's satisfaction.

Celler has informed you that Beyer's payments must be in cash, since she plans on not reporting this as income to the IRS.

a. Is there anything you should do, ethically, before you draft the contract? Or is there anything that might keep you from drafting the contract altogether? Be prepared to explain briefly in class.

b. As you draft the contract, you decide that before you deliver it to the parties you are going to offer Celler $4,500 for the car, cash payment in full at the time of delivery. Is there anything unethical about that? Suppose you were representing only Celler? Be prepared to explain briefly in class.

c. Draft the contract.

Exercise 17: Public Drinking Ordinance

City Council Member Carrie Nations is concerned about what she calls *public drinking* and wants you to draft an ordinance to prohibit it. Upon further inquiry, you discover that her concern includes derelicts who sit in doorways and on sidewalks guzzling cheap wine, sports fans who bring and consume beer at the city baseball stadium (inside the stadium and in the parking lot), kids who congregate at night for drinking parties in remote corners of shopping mall parking lots (despite efforts of mall security to evict them), and the denizens of abandoned houses and weedy vacant lots who are dealing in drugs ("this will give the police an alternative reason for arresting these scumbags," she says).

"What about the concession stand at the Mellon Center for the Performing Arts?" you ask. "They sell wine. Do you want to prohibit that?" "Of course not," she snaps. "They have a license to sell liquor."

"What about the Dessau Motor Speedway?" you ask. "They drink in the stands and parking lot there all the time." "That is private property," she replies. "If Charlie Dessau doesn't care, I don't care."

"Will the police actually have to witness a person drinking the alcohol?" you ask. She thinks about that for a moment and replies, "No, that would make proof too hard. Make possession enough. Or just figure out something, for the love of Pete! Isn't that what we pay you for?"

Prepare the requested ordinance.

Exercise 18: Age Discrimination Waiver

John Barleycorn is the Yard Superintendent at the Birmingham rail yards of the Somerset & Dorset Railway Company. Barleycorn has a high school degree. As Yard Superintendent, Barleycorn has had considerable responsibility for the business, employment, and other contractual affairs of the Company. Barleycorn has always been a good employee.

However, the Company has decided to computerize the rail car switching operations at its Birmingham facility. Barleycorn is not familiar with the computer technology that will be used and has indicated no willingness to try to learn it.

The Company has thus decided that it must terminate Barleycorn. Since Barleycorn is not being terminated *for cause*, he will be entitled to severance pay in the amount of one month's salary.

The man who will replace Barleycorn is 37 years old. He has the necessary expertise to supervise a computerized operation.

Although the Company believes that it has a legitimate and nondiscriminatory reason for replacing Barleycorn, it is fearful that Barleycorn will bring an age discrimination law suit. It has thus asked you draft a waiver. The company is willing to pay Barleycorn an extra two weeks' pay (in addition to the regular severance pay) in return for this waiver.

Using the substantive checklist you developed in Exercise 2, prepare the necessary waiver.

Exercise 19: Independent Contractor Agreement

Terra Firma Real Estate Management Company, Inc., manages commercial real estate properties throughout the Southeast -- shopping centers, strip malls, office buildings, apartment buildings, warehouses, and the like. Its headquarters are at 1861 Peachtree Lane, Atlanta, GA 39901 The Company is very dependent on computer technology. In its headquarters office it has 76 desktop computers, which are networked and connected to all the usual peripherals -- CD-ROM towers, printers, scanners, FAX machines, and others. The Company also has on-site computers and various peripherals at most of the properties it manages. The Company uses over 35 different software programs and operates its own web page.

Needless to say, something is always going wrong with the hardware (with the causes ranging from a defect in the product to user abuse), the computers often refuse to *talk* to the various peripherals, and the net suffers from a lot of *down time*. Employees require training. Specific application questions are always coming up. Data is sometimes *lost* and must be retrieved. And the web page seems to need constant updating and attention.

Over the years, the Company has relied primarily on the service personnel of the various hardware and software vendors to take care of these problems. But this has proved to be expensive, slow, and unsatisfactory. It has also used several independent computer service companies, with a resulting hodge-podge of systems and incompatible solutions. Occasionally, employees who purport to have expertise have fixed (or attempted to fix) a problem on an emergency basis. The Company has thus decided that it needs to hire its own computer expert to keep the entire company-wide computer system running efficiently. It estimates that on average it would have 20 to 25 hours of work for such a person each week, including travel time to locations out of Atlanta.

Dorothy Kham, known to her friends as Dot, recently graduated from Georgia Tech with a masters degree in computer technology and engineering. She has set herself up as a computer consultant, doing business as Kham Computer Technologies, at 1289-b Butler Terrace, Atlanta, GA 39902. She charges $65 per hour. She has heard that Terra Firma is looking for someone to attend to its computer needs and has offered her services. Terra Firma is impressed and wants to retain her, but only as an independent contractor and not as an employee.

It wants you to draft an appropriate contract. The following article contains suggestions regarding content.

Drafting Effective Independent Contractor Agreements

Kenneth A. Jenero & Phillip M. Schreiber*

. . . .

This article discusses the key provisions that should be incorporated into or omitted from an independent contractor agreement. To a great extent, these provisions track the 20 factors used by the IRS to distinguish between an employer-employee and an independent contractor relationship. Indeed, a preliminary step before drafting an independent contractor agreement is to evaluate the actual

*23 Employee Relations Law Journal, No. 4, p. 127 (Spring 1998) [footnotes omitted]. Copyright © Employee Relations Law Journal 1998. Used by permission.

or proposed relationship between the parties, in light of the IRS's 20 factors, to determine whether an independent contractor relationship exists, in fact. If not, the relationship may need to be restructured to more closely resemble a true independent contractor relationship. If that is not feasible, the employer may choose to recognize the relationship as one between an employer and an employee, or at least make informed decisions about the risks associated with maintaining the "independent contractor" relationship.

KEY PROVISIONS OF INDEPENDENT CONTRACTOR AGREEMENTS

In drafting an independent contractor agreement, it is necessary to dispense with the employer-employee framework. The agreement should define a relationship which the law recognizes as an independent contractor relationship. Terminology such as "employer" and "employee" should be discarded. Instead, the agreement should use alternative terms such as "client" and "contractor." The agreement should reflect that the client is interested only in the result to be accomplished by the contractor's work, and not in the manner and details by which the result will be accomplished. Consistent therewith, the terms of the agreement should emphasize the client's lack of behavioral and financial control over the contractor with respect to such matters as when, where, and how the work is to be done; the hours of work or schedule that must be followed; the tools, materials, and other equipment to be used; the reports to be submitted, and the contractor's ability to work for other clients at the same time. Other provisions of the agreement should protect the client against losses and liabilities that might arise out of an independent contractor relationship. The key provisions are discussed below.

The Parties

The agreement should first identify the parties. This identification should include the names and addresses of the parties, and a brief statement of the capacity in which each party is entering into the agreement. For example, the agreement could state:

> This independent contractor agreement is entered into by and between Joe Smith, an individual who resides at 1212 North Elm Street, Chicago, Illinois (hereinafter referred to as "Contractor"), and ABC Corp., an Illinois corporation with its principal place of business at 2121 South Oak Street, Chicago, Illinois (hereinafter referred to as "Client").

Nature of the Relationship

The agreement should specify the nature of the parties' relationship. The agreement should clearly state that the parties intend to create an independent contractor relationship and that they do not intend to create an employer-employee relationship. For example, the agreement might provide: "It is understood and agreed that Contractor is an independent contractor and not an employee, agent, joint venturer, or partner of Client." Although such a provision will not be binding on the courts or the IRS, it is indicative of both parties' intent.

Services to be Performed

Provisions setting forth the services to be performed by the independent contractor also should be included in the agreement. The specific tasks or projects for which the independent contractor is retained, and when they are to be completed, should be specified. For example, the agreement could state: "Contractor has been retained to install the XYZ computer software system at Client's principal place of business and such installation shall be completed by no later than December 31, 1997."

Care should be taken to avoid retaining an independent contractor to perform services that are identical or substantially similar to those performed by the client's regular employees in the normal course of the client's business. When an individual's services are so integrated into a company's operations that the success or failure of the business depends on those services to an appreciable degree, the individual performing the services normally will be assumed to be subject to direction and control by the owners of the business, and thus, to be an employee rather than an independent contractor.

Degree of Control

The agreement should not specify how or where the tasks or projects are to be worked on or completed. These decisions generally should be left to the independent contractor's discretion. Likewise, the independent contractor should be allowed to set his or her own hours of work. As noted above, the degree of control retained by the client over the details and manner of the contractor's work is the ultimate determinate of the nature of the relationship. Provisions that specify the methods by which tasks or projects are to be worked on or completed, or state where or when work should be done, are considered by the IRS to be indicative of an employer-employee relationship.

In order to avoid this pitfall, language similar to the following might be used in this agreement:

> Contractor shall determine the methods, details, and means of providing the above-referenced services. Client is interested only in the result to be accomplished by Contractor and shall have no right to control the manner or determine the method by which such services are provided.

Training, Instructions, and Reports

The agreement should provide that the contractor will not be subject to the client's training or instructions with respect to the methods, details, or means of providing the agreed-upon services. Instead, the agreement may provide that the client is relying on the contractor's own training and expertise to perform the services in a professional and workman-like manner, and specifically require the contractor to warrant his or her skills and expertise in the area. Similarly, the agreement should not require the contractor to provide regular written or oral reports on the status of the services being performed. Periodic reporting requirements are considered by the IRS to be indicative of an employer-employee relationship.

Compensation and Benefits

The agreement should provide that the independent contractor is to be compensated on a per task, per project, or fee basis rather than on a weekly, biweekly, or monthly basis. Regularly scheduled payments are viewed by the IRS as indicative of an employer-employee relationship. Along the same vein, the agreement should provide that the independent contractor is required to submit periodic invoices in order to receive payment. Payments to the independent contractor should not be made by the client's payroll department. Rather, they should be made by the accounts payable department. In addition, the agreement should specify that no payroll or employment taxes will be withheld or paid with respect to any payments to the contractor. Finally, the agreement should expressly state that the contractor, as such, is not entitled to any of the benefits provided by the client to its employees.

Such provisions might take the following form:

Contractor shall be paid three hundred dollars ($300.00) upon completion of each Project. Contractor shall submit monthly invoices to Client by the 5th of each month itemizing each project completed during the prior month. Client shall remit to Contractor payment for all properly received invoices within fifteen (15) days of receipt. No payroll or employment taxes of any kind (including, but not limited to, FICA, FUTA, federal or state personal income taxes, state disability insurance taxes, and state unemployment insurance taxes) shall be withheld or paid with respect to any payments to Contractor.

Because Contractor is not an employee of Client, Contractor acknowledges that he is not entitled to any benefits paid by Client to its employees, including, but not limited to, vacation pay, holiday pay, profit sharing, health insurance, unemployment insurance, and workers' compensation insurance.

Costs and Expenses

If the client bears the costs and expenses associated with providing the services, the IRS may view such an arrangement as evidence of an employer-employee relationship. Accordingly, the agreement should provide that the independent contractor will be responsible for his or her own expenses, including, but not limited to, the costs of any tools, equipment, and materials that may be needed to complete the tasks or projects. If the parties wish to provide that the client will reimburse the contractor for certain expenses, then those expenses should be specified in the agreement. The agreement should require the independent contractor to submit expense reports for any reimbursable expenses.

The agreement should further provide that the independent contractor will be solely responsible for compensating any individuals hired to assist him or her in completing the tasks or projects (that is, subcontractors or employees). Provisions for indemnification by the independent contractor to the client with respect to these expenses also should be included in the agreement. These various provisions identify the contractor's investment in the facilities and personnel he or she will use to perform the agreed-upon services and, thus, are consistent with the existence of an independent contractor relationship.

Such provisions could read as follows:

> Except as stated herein, Contractor shall be fully and solely responsible for all costs and expenses incident to the services furnished to Client under this Agreement, including, but not limited to, all costs of training, tools, equipment, materials, fees, licenses, fines,

bonds, taxes (including, but not limited to, federal, state and local income taxes, FICA, FUTA, workers' compensation, and unemployment insurance taxes), and all of Contractor's other costs of doing business. Contractor is fully and solely responsible for all costs and expenses (including, but not limited to, compensation, benefits, federal, state and local income taxes, FICA, FUTA, workers' compensation, and unemployment insurance taxes) for any of his employees or other persons hired to assist him in providing services to Client under this Agreement. Contractor agrees to fully indemnify Client for any and all costs and expenses of Contractor that Client is required to pay.

Should Contractor be required to travel to complete the project, Client will reimburse Contractor for the cost of any pre-approved airline ticket purchase (but no other travel expenses). Any reimbursement request must be submitted with an expense report within fifteen (15) days of purchasing the airline ticket.

Limitation of Authority

Employees typically are vested with authority to bind their employer to contracts. To avoid any confusion along these lines, an independent contractor agreement should clearly provide that the contractor lacks any such authority. For example, the agreement might state: "Contractor shall not have any authority to act on or behalf of, or to bind, Client in any manner, except as expressly authorized in writing by Client's President."

Insurance

To further protect the client against liability to third parties for the acts of the contractor, the agreement should mandate that the contractor maintain a policy of insurance in an appropriate amount to provide coverage for injuries or damage to third parties. An appropriate provision may be phrased as follows:

> Contractor agrees to maintain a policy of insurance in the minimum amount of five hundred thousand dollars ($500,000) to cover any claims arising out of or in any way related to any act or failure to act by Contractor, including, but not limited to, all claims relating to the injury or death of any person or damage to any property, and to fully protect Client and its shareholders, directors, officers, employees, and agents from and against any and all liability, losses, payments, and expenses incurred or imposed in connection therewith.

Restrictions on Work for Others

Employees typically are required to work full time and exclusively for their employer. Thus, an independent contractor agreement should not specify that the contractor is to devote his or her full time to the client. The IRS views such a provision as indicative of an employer-employee relationship. For the same reason, provisions that require the independent contractor to provide his or her services exclusively to the client should be avoided. Ideally, the independent contractor should have his or her own business name and office, advertise his or her services to the public, and retain the right to perform services for others during the term of the agreement.

Protection Against Unfair Competition

Depending on the nature of the working relationship between the client and the independent contractor, it may be important for the client to protect itself from unfair competition by the contractor. For example, an independent contractor agreement may contain a restrictive covenant that limits the ability of the contractor to solicit business from or sell products or services to the client's customers that are competitive with the client's business, products, or services. This is particularly important where the contractor has had access to the client's customers in the performance of his or her services under the agreement. In addition, the agreement may prohibit the independent contractor from "pirating" the client's employees. These restrictive provisions generally must be of reasonable duration and geographic scope. Their enforceability will vary from state to state. Sample language might read as follows:

> During the term of this Agreement and during the one (1) year period immediately following the date of termination of this Agreement, Contractor shall not, directly or indirectly, by any means or devices whatsoever, in any individual or representative capacity, solicit business from, or sell products, or services to, any customer of Client, where such business, products, or services would be or are in any way competitive with Client's business, products, or services. For purposes of this paragraph, the term "customer of Client" shall mean a past or present customer of Client to which

> Contractor provided services under the terms of this agreement at any time during the one (1) year period immediately preceding the date of termination of this Agreement.
>
> During the term of this Agreement and during the one (1) year period immediately following the date of termination of this Agreement, Contractor shall not, directly or indirectly, by any means or devices whatsoever, in any individual or representative capacity, (a) hire, employ, or attempt to hire or employ any employee of Client, or (b) otherwise solicit, request, entice, or induce any employee of Client to terminate his or her employment with Client.

Protection of Confidential Information

If an independent contractor is privy to confidential information or trade secrets, steps should be taken in the agreement to prohibit, and protect the client against, the inadvertent or intentional use or disclosure of such information. Such provisions could read as follows:

> Contractor acknowledges that in the performance of this Agreement, he may be granted otherwise prohibited access to trade secrets and other information, whether or not reduced to writing, patented, copyrighted or trademarked, that is confidential in nature and of great proprietary and competitive value to client (hereinafter referred to as "Confidential Information"). Contractor shall not, at any time, whether during or after the term of this Agreement, directly or

indirectly, by any means or devices whatsoever, divulge, use, or permit the use of any Confidential Information, except as required in the performance of this Agreement for purposes of Client's business. Without limiting the foregoing, upon termination of this Agreement, Contractor shall turn over to Client all Confidential Information (including copies and duplicates thereof) in his possession or otherwise subject to his control. It is understood and agreed that Contractor will not retain any copy, duplicate, or note memorializing any such Confidential Information.

Term of the Relationship

The IRS views a continuous relationship as indicative of one between an employer and employee. Therefore, when feasible, an independent contractor agreement should specify a fixed term for its duration. For example: "This Agreement will terminate on December 31, 1997." Alternatively, the agreement should set forth events that will cause it to terminate, such as the completion of the subject project.

Termination of the Relationship

The right of discharge is held by an employer and allows the employer to exercise a degree of control over its employees. Therefore, an independent contractor agreement should not discuss discharge. Instead, the agreement should address termination of the relationship.

Here again, however, care should be taken. If the parties have the right to terminate the relationship at will and without any consequences, then the IRS may view such a relationship as one between an employer and employee. On the other hand, provisions which permit the client to terminate the relationship only if the contractor is failing to perform under the agreement, or which impose liability on the contractor for any incomplete tasks or projects, are considered indicative of an independent contractor relationship. A suggested provision might state:

> Client may terminate this Agreement at any time for cause, including, but not limited to, Contractor's breach of any of the terms of this Agreement. If this Agreement is terminated by either party prior to completion of the Project, then Contractor shall be liable to Client for all costs and expenses incurred by Client in completing the Project.

Other Provisions

An independent contractor agreement may provide that the contractor is prohibited from duplicating or removing materials belonging to the client, or that any such materials borrowed by the contractor must be returned at the conclusion of the relationship. Likewise, the agreement may provide the client with the rights to any intellectual property created by the contractor during the course of his service to the client. "Boilerplate" provisions found in virtually all written agreements also may be included in an independent contractor agreement. These include common provisions relating to amendments and modifications, assignability, governing law, the venue where disputes will be adjudicated, arbitration, severability of the agreement's provisions, and non-waiver of rights.

CONCLUSION

This article has identified key provisions to include in and omit from independent contractor agreements. (A "Summary of the Dos and Don'ts of Independent Contractor Agreements" appears in the accompanying chart.) . . . [I]ndependent contractor agreements . . . have value as documents which memorialize the parties' understanding regarding the nature of the relationship; establish a framework for the parties' relationship which, if followed, will maximize the likelihood of an independent contractor determination; and may have a deterrent effect on claims predicated on an alleged employer-employee relationship. In the final analysis, an independent contractor agreement will be enforced as such only when it, in fact, defines the relationship that actually exists between the parties.

THE DOS AND DON'TS OF INDEPENDENT CONTRACTOR AGREEMENTS

- Do identify the parties in their proper capacity.
- Do specify the nature of the relationship as one between a client and independent contractor.
- Do set forth the services to be performed by the independent contractor.
- Do leave the methods and details of performance to the independent contractor.
- Do specify that the client is interested only in the result to be accomplished by the independent contractor.

- Do provide that the client is relying on the independent contractor's own training and expertise to perform the services in a professional manner.

- Do require the contractor to warrant his skills and expertise in the area in which he is performing services.

- Do pay the independent contractor on a per project or fee basis.

- Do specify that the independent contractor is required to submit periodic invoices in order to receive payment.

- Do specify that no payroll or employment taxes will be withheld or paid with respect to any payments to the independent contractor

- Do specify that the independent contractor is not entitled to any benefits provided to the client's employees.

- Do provide that the independent contractor is responsible for all costs and expenses associated with providing the services.

- Do specify the expenses, if any, for which the independent contractor will be reimbursed and provide for the submission of supporting expense reports.

- Do provide that the independent contractor is solely responsible for compensating any individuals hired to assist in completing the services.

- Do limit the independent contractor's authority to bind the client.

- Do require the independent contractor to provide insurance to protect the client against liability to third parties.

- Do provide restrictive covenants prohibiting solicitation of the client's customers and "pirating" of the client's employees.

- Do protect the client from inadvertent or intentional use or disclosure of its confidential information.

- Do specify a fixed term for the relationship or set forth events which will cause the relationship to terminate.

- Do hold the independent contractor liable for unfinished work upon termination of the relationship.

- Don't use terms such as "employer" and "employee."

- Don't specify the hours of work or schedule to be followed by the independent contractor.

- Don't specify how or where the services are to be performed by the independent contractor .

- Don't subject the independent contractor to

the client's training or instructions with respect to the method and details of providing the services.

- Don't require the independent contractor to provide periodic reports regarding the status of the work.

- Don't require the independent contractor to work exclusively for the client.

- Don't require the independent contractor to devote full time to the client's project.

- Don't provide for the client to supply the independent contractor with tools, equipment, or other materials.

- Don't allow the independent contractor to bind or act on behalf of the client.

- Don't provide for a continuous term.

- Don't provide that the agreement may be terminated by either party at will, and without consequence to either party.

Exercise 20: Confidentiality Agreement

You represent the Rearden Steel Company (listed on the New York Stock Exchange as "RSC"). Jack Rearden, President and major stockholder, has told you that he has received an enquiry from Carbolic Fabricators, through its CEO, John Galt, suggesting an interest in purchasing Rearden's stock. If the price is right, Rearden might be willing to sell. Galt, however, wants to do a thorough investigation of Rearden Steel before it proceeds. This will necessarily involve making Carbolic personnel privy to confidential information about Rearden's finances, production techniques, customer lists, and other matters. Rearden wants to make sure that this information remains confidential. He has asked you to draft a confidentiality agreement.

a. Using the following article for guidance, construct a substantive-content check list of matters that should, from the *disclosing party's* perspective, be included in such a document.

b. Then construct a list of matters that, from the *interested party's* perspective, should be deleted from or added to that list.

c. Finally, draft an agreement for Rearden.

Drafting and Negotiating Effective Confidentiality Agreements

By Brian D. Bowden*

Confidentiality agreements create the contractual framework within which one party discloses to another confidential and proprietary information. These agreements typically arise in the context of business acquisitions or dispositions, in which the disclosure of such information is necessary or desirable to enable substantive discussions regarding a potential transaction to proceed. Although confidentiality provisions often are included in basic transactional documents, a free-standing agreement is preferable because (a) it is more comprehensive and thus may better protect the interests of the disclosing party, (b) its enforceability is not dependent on that of a more-encompassing document that includes other, unrelated provisions, and (c) it may be entered into before the parties have discussed any substantive issues regarding the proposed transaction. In addition, the use of a separate agreement requires the parties to focus on an important subject that often is given insufficient consideration.

Because most, if not all, of the obligations in a confidentiality agreement typically burden the recipient of the information (the "interested party"), the interested party generally favors the shortest and least-comprehensive agreement possible. Conversely, it is incumbent on the disclosing party to ensure that the agreement provides adequate protection in all relevant areas. Although the length of the agreement and its level of detail will vary depending on the relative sophistication of, and the degree

---

*59 Texas Bar Journal 524 (1996).

of familiarity and trust between, the parties, it is possible to provide a disclosing party with effective protection in a concise agreement. This article presents the typical, salient provisions of a confidentiality agreement from the perspective of each party, together with commonly-negotiated compromises. . . .

Definition of Information

Central to the agreement is the definition of the information to which the agreement pertains. Not surprisingly, the disclosing party will want to define "information" as broadly as possible. A comprehensive definition should include all information actually disclosed, whether before or after the execution of the agreement, whether tangible or intangible, and in whatever form or medium provided, as well as all information generated by the interested party or by its representatives that contains, reflects, or is derived from the provided information. The definition should also include the fact that the confidentiality agreement exists and that discussions between the parties concerning the proposed transaction are taking place. Alternatively, the parties may choose to prohibit disclosure of these facts in a separate paragraph of the agreement. In either case, the interested party should make the obligation with respect to the nondisclosure of this portion of the information reciprocal.

The interested party should seek to exclude the following from the definition of "information":

(a) Information that is or becomes publicly available other than through acts by the interested party or by its representatives in violation agreement. In negotiating the precise language of this exclusion, it is important to the interested party that the term "publicly available" is used rather than "in the public domain," which connotes legal entitlement to use. The interested party also should avoid a requirement that the information be "generally known by" the public, as this language imposes an additional and difficult evidentiary hurdle to overcome. The interested party also will want to ensure that the acts negating the exclusion are only those done in violation of the agreement.

(b) Information that is already in the interested party's possession at the time of its disclosure by the disclosing party. The disclosing party may require that the interested party's possession be "rightful" or "lawful," but the interested party should avoid these terms because they signify legal entitlement to use. The disclosing party also may require that prior possession be "evidenced by the interested party's written records," which restricts the types of evidence that the interested party may use to support its reliance on the exclusion. Although, as a practical matter, it will be difficult for an interested party to avail itself successfully of the exclusion without written evidence, there is no conceptual justification for this restriction.

(c) Information that is disclosed to the interested party by a third party who, to the interested party's knowledge, is not prohibited from disclosing the information pursuant to a confidentiality agreement with the disclosing party. The disclosing party will prefer (i) to omit the knowledge qualifier so that the interested party guarantees that the source of the information was, in fact, entitled to disclose it and (ii) to expand the source of the prohibition on disclosure to any fiduciary, contractual, or other duty to any person. A well-accepted compromise is to impose on the interested party only a duty of due inquiry as to the right of the third party to disclose the information, but to accept the disclosing party's broader scope of the source of the prohibition on disclosure.

Subject to the negotiation of precise language, the three categories of exclusion set forth above are almost universally accepted. There are, however, two additional categories of exclusion that the interested party should attempt to obtain that may not be acceptable to the disclosing party.

(d) Information that the interested party develops or derives without the aid, application, or use of the furnished information. Although this exclusion is unobjectionable in concept, the disclosing party often perceives it as too broad and subject to abuse. Because of this perception, and because the exclusion imposes a difficult evidentiary burden on the interested party in any event, the disclosing party's position usually prevails.

(e) Information that the interested party is advised by legal counsel is required to be disclosed by law or by legal process. The disclosing party often objects to this category because the agreement typically contains a separate paragraph on legal process. From the interested party's perspective, however, the exclusion is desirable because it insulates the interested party from liability regardless of whether the interested party follows precisely the detailed requirements of the legal process paragraph. It is particularly important that the interested party include the words "is advised by legal counsel" to avoid becoming a guarantor of the legal obligation to disclose the information to a court or other judicial or administrative body.

Permitted Use of the Information

The agreement should specify the purpose for which the interested party may use the information and should specifically prohibit any other use. The best approach is simply to recite that the information may be used only to assist the interested party in evaluating the proposed transaction, which the agreement may describe with the desired degree of specificity. This provision is usually not controversial, but the interested party should avoid ambiguous language regarding prohibited uses, such as "use in any way detrimental to the disclosing party."

Permitted Discloses

It is important to both parties that the agreement establish clearly the categories of persons to whom the interested party may disclose the information and to what extent the interested party will be liable for acts by any such persons in violation of the agreement. The agreement should define such persons (who typically include officers, directors, partners, employees, affiliates, agents, and representatives) as the "representatives," or some similar term, of the interested party. To insulate the interested party more effectively from liability, the interested party should omit from this definition persons who are not within its control and have them enter into separate and independent confidentiality agreements with the disclosing party. Potential co-investors, in particular, should be excluded because they are not agents of the interested party and their interests may be inconsistent. By defining "representatives" generically, the term also can be applied to the disclosing party with respect to its obligations under the agreement.

Following a description of permitted disclosees, the agreement typically provides that the interested party will provide the information only to those of its representatives who (i) need it to assist the interested party in evaluating the proposed transaction, (ii) are provided with a copy of the confidentiality agreement, and (iii) agree to be bound by the confidentiality agreement to the same extent as if they were signatories thereto. The disclosing party should include a provision making the interested party fully liable for acts by its representatives in violation of the agreement and may also wish to require a written undertaking of the representatives to be bound by the confidentiality agreement, but this latter requirement is burdensome to the interested party and is not usually imposed. Similarly, the interested party may attempt to exculpate itself from lability for the acts of its representatives once it has complied with the specified conditions, but this attempt is rarely successful. The disclosing party may include an additional requirement that the interested party take all reasonable measures to prevent its representatives from violating the agreement. Assuming that the interested party is willing to agree to this in concept, the interested party should strike the word "all" so that it may more easily defend its actions to prevent such disclosure if they prove to be unsuccessful.

Return of the Information

The agreement usually obligates the interested party to return the information once the interested party has determined not to pursue the proposed transaction, or anytime at the request of the disclosing party. The interested party should (a) obligate itself to return the information only upon the disclosing party's request, so that the disclosing party has the burden of initiating the return process, (b) require the disclosing party's request to be in writing, and (c) be permitted to destroy information not furnished by the disclosing party rather than deliver it to the disclosing party. The disclosing party reasonably may require that an officer of the interested party certify the destruction in writing, and that the furnished information be returned to it within a specified length of time, commonly five days after receipt of the notice.

Legal Process Seeking Disclosure Of the Information

The disclosing party should obligate the interested party to follow certain procedures if it is requested to disclose any of the information pursuant to legal process. As typically drafted by the disclosing party, the agreement provides that, in such event, the interested party (a) must give the disclosing party as much notice as possible to enable the disclosing party to attempt to avoid the disclosure, (b) must use its best efforts to cooperate with the disclosing party in any such attempt, and (c) may disclose only that part of the information that, in the written opinion of its legal counsel, it is required to disclose. The interested party should (a) avoid any requirement that the legal process be "valid" or that the subpoena or order be issued by a court of "competent jurisdiction," as these are legal determinations that the interested party will not necessarily be in a position to make, (b) ensure that the opinion of its counsel is not required to be written to avoid the expense and difficulty of obtaining a formal legal opinion quickly, (c) agree to use reasonable, rather than best, efforts to ensure that the confidentiality of the information is maintained, and require that all such efforts be at the sole cost and expense of the disclosing party, and (d) avoid any requirement that the interested party be subject imminently to contempt or other penalty before disclosing the information.

Disclaimer of Accuracy and Completeness

The disclosing party often includes in the agreement a disclaimer as to the accuracy and completeness of the information. While this is usually acceptable, the interested party should seek to include the disclosing party's representation that it believes in good faith that the furnished information is in fact accurate. The disclosing party likely will be more reluctant to represent that the furnished information is complete.

Attorneys' Fees

Because the interested party has the great majority of the obligations in the agreement, the disclosing party will want to make the interested party responsible for the disclosing party's costs and expenses in the event of a breach or threatened breach of the agreement. The interested party should (a) make the obligation reciprocal, (b) limit the obligation to those expenses actually and reasonably incurred by the prevailing party in successful litigation, so that the disclosing party must prevail in court to recover under this provision and so that investigatory and other pre-litigation costs and expenses are excluded, and (c) delete the rcference to threatened breaches.

No Obligation To Proceed with the Proposed Transaction

To protect itself against potential claims that it has agreed to consummate the proposed transaction with the interested party as a result of, among other things, the execution of the confidentiality agreement, the disclosing party should include a specific statement that, until the execution and delivery of a definitive agreement, the parties are under no obligation with respect to the proposed transaction by virtue of the confidentiality agreement or of any other written or oral understanding or agreement, except with respect to the matters specifically addressed in the confidentiality agreement. This provision should be acceptable to the interested party if it does not include blanket waivers of claims against the disclosing party.

Waiver of Right To Jury Trial

The disclosing party should require the interested party to waive its right to a jury trial. From the perspective of the disclosing party, who is the likely plaintiff in any court proceeding, the waiver serves to expedite the trial and to increase the likelihood that any technical issues, particularly with respect to the nature of the information and to the damages flowing from breach of the agreement, will be understood fully and given adequate consideration. The interested party, of course, should avoid this waiver. Even if the disclosing party prevails on this point, however, the disclosing party should include a severability clause in the agreement to protect itself against a court finding that the waiver is unenforceable on public policy grounds.

Representation of Rightful Disclosure

The interested party should include in the agreement (a) the disclosing party's representation that it is entitled to disclose the information, and (b) an indemnity for any breach of such representation. This provision is particularly important when the information relates to another party who is not a signatory to the confidentiality agreement and there is no clear and substantiated agency relationship between the disclosing party and such other party. This issue typically arises when the disclosing party is an investment banker who has been retained to assist a client with the disposition of its business or assets.

. . . .

Prohibition On Solicitation of Employees

Depending on the particular circumstances, the disclosing party may want to prohibit the interested party from hiring any of the disclosing party's employees for a specified period of time. The interested party should attempt to limit the prohibition (a) to the solicitation, but not the hiring, of key employees who were identified by the interested party pursuant to its evaluation of the proposed transaction, and (b) to personal, as opposed to general, solicitation. Acceptable time periods for the prohibition typically range from six months to two years.

Forum And Venue Provisions

If a disclosing party is entering into agreements with one or more interested parties in different geographical locations, it is a good idea to provide for exclusive forum and venue in a court of its choice and to include the interested party's consent to personal jurisdiction and waiver of its right to invoke the inconvenient forum objection. The interested party may lessen the effect of these provisions simply by making the forum and venue selections non-exclusive.

Right to Equitable Remedies

Disclosing parties commonly include the interested party's acknowledgment that the disclosing party will be entitled to specific performance and other equitable remedies in the event of a breach or threatened breach of the agreement without the posting of any bond and without proof of actual damages. Because equitable remedies are by their nature within judicial discretion, however, the effectiveness of this provision is questionable. Rather than arguing for deletion of the entire provision, an interested party may prefer to nullify its effect simply by stating that the disclosing party will be entitled to *seek* equitable remedies. Although the effect of this change should be transparent to most readers, counsel to disclosing parties have accepted it more often than one might expect. In any event, the interested party should attempt to delete the references to the posting of bond and to proof of damages.

. . . .

Term of the Agreement

As typically drafted by the disclosing party, the agreement specifies no term, and this position should prevail on the merits. A specified term is unjustified for information that consists of trade secrets and, to the extent that it consists of financial information, such information will become stale over time in any event. In addition, financial information pertaining to a public company will be publicly-disclosed on a periodic basis pursuant to securities laws requirements. Finally, the disclosing party justifiably will not want any contractual time limit on its remedies.

Conclusion

Too often parties give insufficient consideration to maintaining the confidentiality of proprietary information in the rush to negotiate and complete a proposed transaction. Careful attention to this issue at the beginning of discussions will better protect the disclosing party, in particular, if the relationship between the parties becomes adversarial.

Exercise 21: Employment Contract

Barbara Halmark Webster, owner of Webster Wire & Cable Company, Inc., recently terminated her office manager. It had been an unsatisfactory relationship, because they were in constant disagreement over job duties, what benefits the manager was entitled to, and the scope of her authority. Before Webster hires a new manager, she wants to have an employment contract prepared that will forestall these problems. She has asked you to draft one.

You met with her, went through the checklist you prepared in Exercise 3.a., and took the following notes.

Webster Wire & Cable Company, Inc., PPB = 8867 Airport Blvd., Austin, Texas 79703. Family owned, closed corporation (Texas). Barbara Halmark Webster, President.

Manufactures and fabricates various grades of industrial wire, some by special order. Has clients in Texas, Okla, and La. Production mgr -- in charge of production, 27 employees. Sales mgr -- supervises 6 sales persons. Head of shipping --handles all shipments and supervises 2 loading-dock workers. Maintenance chief -- with crew of 3, repairs and maintains machinery. These department heads have contracts. Everyone else is at-will.

Job title -- office manager.

Job duties -- Hire/fire/supervise 1 receptionist/secretary, 2 clerical employees, and a bookkeeper. Must have computer skills (various word processing, spread sheet, and data base software programs -- find out specifics, Webster doesn't have a clue as to what they use). Arrange for office cleaning and maintenance (currently using a service). Be in charge of all office equipment and supplies; keep personnel and payroll records -- tax withholding, social sec., and medicare withholding. Arrange for computer support services (currently use Mike Roe Soft Computer Consultants & Technicians, Inc.). Handle advertising and public relations (currently limited to sponsoring a girls softball team). Act as personal secretary to Webster. Assist production mgr, sales mgr. and shipping in handling various paperwork, as needed. Otherwise serve as "girl Friday" (advise client not to use that term). Reserve right to modify duties, as needed.

Full time.

$42,000 per year, payable in semimonthly payments.

Vacation -- 3 weeks each 12 months (measured from date of hire); no carry over. No more than 2 weeks at a time. No less than 3 days at a time. 2 weeks notice to Webster and approval.

Holidays -- Christmas day, New Years day, 4th July, Thanksgiving, either Friday before or Monday after Easter.

FMLA leave -- policy described in "Family and Medical Leave Act Leave Act Policy" (which you drafted for her earlier). Incorporate by reference.

Other leave (for personal, religious, and other non-FMLA covered purposes) -- without pay, 7 days per year -- one week notice required, except in emergencies.

Insurance -- covered by company's Blue Cross and Blue Shield medical insurance policy. No other insurance.

No retirement plan. Employees urged to have 401(k)s.

Contract will be for one year.

Employer may terminate early under two circumstances. 1) for "cause," including failure to perform job duties satisfactorily, any other breach of this contract, insubordination, refusal to follow instructions, absenteeism (beyond authorized leave), dishonesty, being intoxicated while on the job, etc. 2) Non-"cause" early justifications for terminations include elimination of job position, insolvency, closure of business, sale of business, and for other legitimate economic and business reasons not related to employee's job performance. Employer may terminate at any time and for no reason at all if 2 weeks notice is given and employee is paid a full month's salary as severance pay.

Employee may terminate at any time, provided 2 weeks notice is given.

Contract automatically renews from year to year, unless terminated.

Normal work schedule. Monday-Friday, 9:00 to 5:00, with one hour for lunch. Employee may be expected to work additional hours, including on weekends, if the needs of the business dictate.

No arbitration!

Exercise 22: Apartment Lease

You have gone over the checklist developed for your client in Exercise 3.b. and the interview produced the following information. Some items on the checklist require no information from the client and should be included automatically. If information would be required for a checklist item but none is given, assume that it is unnecessary to include any reference of the matter (for example, these apartments have no out-of-unit storage areas).

You have also learned that the apartments are near the University Law School. The client informs you that most of the tenants, thus, will probably be law students -- who, he notes from experience, have a penchant for wielding "their superficial knowledge of the law like three year olds playing with the Excaliber Sword." Draft the lease agreement with that particular audience in mind.

Client Notes:

Name of Apartment. Collegiate Apartments, 248 Elm Street, Cambridge, Your state.

Landlord: Ronald Hawthorne deTrump, doing business as deTrump Realty, Inc., 1330 South Main Street, Cambridge, Your state.

Apartment Manager & Owner's Agent: Martha Marbles, Apartment 1-A, Collegiate Apartments, 248 Elm Street, Cambridge, Your state.

Appliances: Refrigerator, stove, dishwasher, disposal.

Cable available; tenant pays.

Parking: No campers, boats, trailers, or truck tops may be kept in lot.

Common areas -- laundry room; coin operated. Other areas landlord will maintain are the two stairways, the small lobby where mailboxes are located, the hallways, the parking lot, and the grounds.

Utilities: Landlord pays electrical, gas, water, and garbage fee.

Garbage: Tenants must place general household garbage in dumpster; segregate paper, glass (clear, brown, green), plastic, and aluminum and put them in the bins marked as such.

Term: One year.

Renewal: Automatically renews for one year unless either party gives notice 30-days in advance of termination date.

Grounds for termination: [Advised client that you will incorporate the statutory grounds for termination as part of the contract.]

Security deposit: One month's rent in advance. [Advised client will incorporate the statutory requirements concerning return as part of the contract.]

Terms of rent: $550 per month.

Paid when: First day of the month, unless it is a Saturday, Sunday, or federal holiday, in which case it will be paid the next day. Before 5:00 p.m. Prepayment allowed, no more than one month's rent in advance. More than 5 days late = "breach."

Where: manager's office.

Method: Check or money order; no cash.

Limits on occupancy:

Number: 2 or 3, depending on which apartment. Leave a blank. All permanent residents must be signatories to the lease.

Children: None

Pets: None

Status of tenants: No limits.

Limits on use of premise: Residence only. No loud parties. No water beds.

Landlord's & tenant's obligations concerning maintenance of the property. [Advised client that you will incorporate the statutory requirements as part of the contract.]

Right of entry: [Advised client you will incorporate the statutory rules as part of the contract.]

Assignment: Tenant cannot assign. Landlord may if property is sold; buyer/assignee bound by terms of lease.

Household goods insurance: Responsibility of tenant. Landlord is not liable for any losses.

Exercise 23: No-Smoking Ordinance

TO: Staff Attorney

FROM: Senator Hector Garcia Gonzales, Chair
Public Health & Welfare Committee

RE: Smoking Ban

I want to introduce a bill prohibiting smoking in all public buildings within the state and in public transportation.

I firmly believe that secondary smoke is detrimental to the health, well-being, and comfort of non-smokers and that we have a right to be free of this pestilence while working in or using public facilities. Indeed, non-smokers should not have to run the gauntlet of smoke in order to enter a public building, so I want a smoke-free zone outside the entrances as well.

I am not insensitive to the rights of smokers. Heavens no! Some of them even vote. They should, thus, be allowed to smoke in their own private offices, provided they are enclosed. Also exempt are designated lounges and break areas, provided that there is a separate and equivalent non-smoking area as well. These areas must contain signs indicating whether they are smoking or non-smoking. On the other hand, I think our hospitals should have the option of being totally smoke free in this regard.

Violation of the smoking ban should be a misdemeanor with a fine of $50 per violation.

Please draft a bill for my review. If you have any questions, do not hesitate to give me a call.

Exercise 24: Anti-Stalking Statute

You are an aide to State Representative Sharon C. Hopkins. Several women's advocacy groups have complained that although the state has an anti-stalking statute, the police are reluctant to arrest persons accused of stalking and that several district attorneys have made it quite plain that prosecuting a stalking case is low on their list of priorities. The Senator investigated further and discovered that both the police and the district attorneys say that the stalking statute is virtually incomprehensible and possibly unconstitutional.

a. To help her better understand the existing statute and its possible defects, she has asked you to prepare a written outline and critique (of both style and substance).

The statute is as follows:

Section 16-3-1070. Crime of Stalking.

(A) For purposes of this section:

(1) "Harasses" means a knowing an wilful course of conduct directed at a specific person which seriously alarms, annoys, or harasses the person and which serves no legitimate purpose. The course of conduct must be such as would cause a reasonable person to suffer substantial emotional distress, and must actually cause substantial emotional distress to the person.

(2) "Course of conduct" means a pattern of conduct composed of a series of acts over a period of time, however short, evidencing a continuity of purpose. Constitutionally protected activity is not included within the meaning of "course of conduct."

(3) "A credible threat" means a threat made with the intent and the apparent ability to carry out the threat so as

to cause the person who is the target of the threat to reasonably fear for his safety. The threat must be against the life of, or a threat to cause great bodily injury to, a person.

(B) It is unlawful for a person to wilfully, maliciously, and repeatedly follow or harass another person and make a credible threat with the intent to place that person in reasonable fear of death or great bodily injury. A person who violates the provision of this section is guilty of the crime of stalking which is a misdemeanor and, upon conviction, must be imprisoned not more than one year or fined not more than one thousand dollars, or both.

(C) A person who violate subsection (B) when there is a temporary restraining order or an injunction, or both, in effect prohibiting the behavior described in subsection (B) against the same party is guilty of stalking which is a misdemeanor and, upon conviction, must be imprisoned not more than two years or fined not more than one thousand dollars, or both.

(D) A person who is convicted of a second or subsequent offense for a violation of subsection (B) within seven years of a prior conviction under subsection (B) against the same victim and involving an act of violence or "a credible threat " of violence as defined in item (3) of subsection (A), is guilty of stalking which is a misdemeanor and, upon conviction, must be imprisoned not more than three years or fined not more than two thousand dollars, or both.

(E) This section does not apply to conduct which occurs during labor picketing.

b. Draft a new anti-stalking statute that cures the problems of the old one and better addresses this troublesome phenomenon.

Exercise 25: Contract For the Sale of Residential Property

Your friends William and Mary Nemo have found a house they want to buy. It is for sale by owner, Daniel Defoe. The Nemo's and Defoe have reached tentative oral agreement over the price and a few other terms. The Nemo's have retained you to prepare a contract of sale, which both parties will review and sign, provided all the terms are satisfactory.

You elicit the following information from your clients:

- The house is at 1877 Lake Road, Gotham City, Yourstate.

- They want title in both their names.

- Defoe wants to take the dining room chandelier with him, but is willing to let them have the John Deere riding lawn mower (he is moving into a high rise apartment and thus has little need for it).

- There is currently a $56,000 lien on the property, which Defoe will satisfy out of the proceeds of the sale.

- The total purchase price is $180,000. The Nemo's are willing to put down $2,500 earnest money at the time the contract is signed. You will act as their escrow agent. They plan to use the proceeds of the sale of their current house for another $35,000 and finance the rest.

- The Nemo's are not willing to pay more than 8% interest or pay more than 2 points to secure a loan. Given the market and their good credit, you expect that they will have no difficulty in obtaining a loan. However, they want their obligation to proceed to be contingent on financing. Defoe wants written assurance of an application for financing from a bank or mortgage company within 10 days of the date of the contract.

- You may assume that any mortgage company will require that the seller provide a survey of the property, a termite letter (stating that the premises are free from active infestation and that there is no structural damage that has been caused by termites), and a heating and air conditioning letter (stating that this equipment is in working order). The sale will be contingent on the seller providing such documents.

- The Nemo's also want to make the sale of their old home, at 647 Ross Avenue, Gotham City, a contingency. Defoe is willing to do this, but he wants to keep his house on the market in case the Nemo's house is not sold by the time of closing. They agreed that if Defoe finds another buyer, Defoe will notify the Nemo's, who will then have five days to either waive the contingency and proceed with the purchase regardless of whether the old home has sold or cancel the contract and have their escrow money returned. However, if they elect to proceed, Defoe wants written assurance from their mortgage company that they can still obtain financing (better put some time limits on this).

- Because the house is over 25 years old, the Nemo's also want to have the house inspected (plumbing, roof, structural) by a licensed building inspector. They will pay for the inspection but want the sale subject to their "satisfaction" of the results of the inspection.

- The parties expect that eight weeks will be a reasonable time to get everything done (the old house sold, financing arranged, the title search, etc.) and thus want the closing date set accordingly.

The Nemo's trust you to include any other necessary provisions and to otherwise protect their interests in this transaction. There is one small problem, however. You have never drafted a contract for the sale of a house and never even bought a house yourself! But your trusty paralegal found the attached article and assured you that it tells you everything you need to know ("Why didn't they teach me this stuff in law school?" you ask yourself -- the answer to which goes beyond the scope of this work). Nevertheless, thusly armed, draft the contract.

DRAFTING THE RESIDENTIAL CONTRACT OF SALE

Caryl A. Yzenbaard*

I. Introduction

The purchase and sale of the family home is probably the greatest investment made by the average family. . . . [T]he objective of this Article is to present an overview or checklist of those areas which must be addressed in the residential contract of sale.

II. The Contract

The contract may take one of several forms depending upon custom and usage in the jurisdiction. It may be a bilateral contract which the seller and buyer sign. Certainly this is an appropriate format, and possibly the preferable one, when attorneys for both the buyer and the seller are involved. [Or], the contract may take the form of an offer by the buyer [which the seller accepts by signing it or by proposing a counter-offer, usually in the form of amendments to the original]. . . .

. . . .

III. The Parties

Although the identification of the parties to the contract is required by the statute of frauds, there is a tendency to understate the importance of getting the signatures of all appropriate parties. Nonetheless, that the

---

*9 William Mitchell L. Rev. 37 (1983) [footnotes omitted].

proper parties sign may be essential in the event of a later breach.

The buyer's attorney should be certain that the seller has been adequately identified and has properly signed the contract. If the property is jointly owned, all owners should be identified and should sign. Failure to have all sellers sign the contract may prevent the enforcement of the contract. If the seller is an individual, the buyer should ascertain the competency of the seller. . . .

. . . .

The buyer should be identified and should sign the contract. The sellers will want to verify that the buyer is an adult and of sound mind. If more than one buyer will be purchasing the property, all should sign in order to avoid potential problems in the event one should die. . . .

Although it is not customary in many areas of the country, the buyers should include a provision regarding how title will be taken. For example, in the case of joint ownership, it might be by tenancy in common, joint tenancy, or tenancy by the entirety. If the buyer has not decided how he or she will take title, a provisions should be included to ensure that notification of how title will be taken is given to the drafter of the deed within a stated period of time. . . .

IV. The Property Description

The contract should include the best available description of the property. Although a description might be sufficient if the property can be identified either by the contract itself or from references therein, some courts either have held that the description in the contract must be as complete as that in the deed or have been otherwise insistent upon complete details. The current practice of using only the street or common address in the contract also creates the risk that the parties will not fully understand which parcel of land is being conveyed. The seller can convey only the land which the seller owns even if that does not correspond to the common description; a discrepancy between the two might either void the contract or frustrate the desires of the parties.

If the street or common address is to be used, it should be noted in the contract that the street or common address will be supplemented by the legal description by which the seller acquired title. A preferable method for obtaining a description is to extract the legal description from a copy of the seller's deed or title opinion and to attach the document to the contract. . . .

It is a maxim that fixtures remain with the real property and personal property does not. Nevertheless, the contract of sale should embody the parties' understanding concerning fixtures and personal property. Any fixture to be removed by the seller should be clearly noted in the contract. A long list of fixtures that will remain on the property should not be included in the contract of sale for two reasons. First, the use of a list creates the risk of omission. For instance, if a fixture is not specifically mentioned, it could be removed. Second, a list gives the appearance that the contract is merely a form and that the client is not getting the personal attention deserved. On the other hand, listing fixtures does serve as notice to laypersons that the items listed will remain on the property. Whether the fixtures are enumerated in the contract or not, the subject should be discussed with the client. Only items to be excluded should be noted in the contract unless the buyer has a special concern about a particular fixture. A fixture to be removed by the seller should be removed prior to the closing.

Unlike fixtures, personal property of the seller does not pass to the buyer unless expressly stated in the contract. No reference should be made in the contract to personal property not to be included in the sale. The buyer's attorney should make certain that the description and price of personal property to be sold are specifically noted. The buyer should receive a bill of sale and an assignment of any warranties or service contracts for the items sold. The seller's attorney should remember that the sale of personal property may carry certain implied warranties which are absent from real property.

V. Encumbrances

The seller should agree to sell the property subject to any and all encumbrances (except for outstanding liens which will be paid prior to or at the closing), zoning ordinances, and encroachments. If there is an outstanding mortgage to be satisfied at the closing, the seller's attorney should include a provision stating that the proceeds of the sale can be used to satisfy the mortgage lien or other liens which may be present. In the absence of such a clause, a buyer might insist that the liens be cleared prior to the closing when the seller might not have the assets.

Commonly a parcel of property is encumbered by easements or restrictions. Obviously, the seller will want to convey the property subject to such easements and restrictions. Provisions to that effect should be included in the contract's property description, deed clause, and the marketable title provisions. The seller should not limit the clause to easements and restrictions of record because the property may well be subject to implied easements or easements acquired by prescription.

The buyer, on the other hand, should not agree to purchase property subject to unknown easements and restrictions. Language limiting encumbrances to easements and restrictions of record will not necessarily adequately protect the buyer. For example, the buyer may not be permitted to use a portion of the home as a separate unit for an aged parent or to have a white picket fence, if valid restrictions of record against such activities exist. In like manner, a tree cherished by the buyer may be cut if it interferes with a recorded easement.

The best solution is for the seller to list all easements and restrictions. If the seller has a copy of the title opinion, abstract of title, or Torrens certificate given at the time of seller's purchase of the property, easements and restrictions of record will be noted therein at least to that date and can be specifically noted in the contract of sale. Typically, however, the seller does not have ready access to such information. In such a case, a provision can be included allowing the buyer a specific period of time for objection, possibly the same period allowed to determine the marketability of title. If no objection is made, the contingency is satisfied and the deed will be conveyed subject either to all easements and restrictions or to those specified in the contract.

Similarly, provision should be made for outstanding encroachments, if any, and zoning ordinances. A seller's attorney should not accept a contract of sale in which the seller represents the current status of the zoning, unless definitely known to the seller. Instead, the contract of sale should provide that the property will be conveyed subject to all zoning ordinances. Zoning ordinances obviously can affect the buyer's use of the property. Because such ordinances, however, do not affect the marketability of title to the property, the buyer must take the property subject to them even if not specified in the contract of sale. Consequently, the buyer's attorney should insert a clause making the buyer's approval of the zoning a condition of purchase. If the buyer's attorney will be doing a title opinion, the attorney should also check the applicable zoning ordinances, which is not a great imposition. Again, the approval period can be the same as that used for ascertaining the marketability of title.

VI. The Deed

The contract of sale should clearly state the type of deed that shall be used. In the absence of such a provision many courts will state that the seller need only give a quitclaim or a bargain and sale deed without covenants. The buyer will probably want a warranty deed so that he may sue for damages if one of the warranties is breached.

. . . .

VII. The Price

The purchase price should be stated clearly. The contract should state the amount of down payment or earnest money to be paid, if any, and the method by which the balance will be financed. If, as will be discussed, the contract is to be contingent upon the buyer securing adequate financing, that condition should be clearly noted.

A down payment accompanying the contract of sale is now commonly required. The most frequently cited reasons for the necessity of a down payment are to provide a remedy for the seller in the event of the buyer's breach and to impress upon the buyer the seriousness of the transaction. The amount of the down payment typically is determined by local custom. Under some circumstances, however, there will be a departure from the custom. For example, a seller may want a larger down payment if the seller is uncertain of the buyer's ability to complete the sale or if the closing will not occur for a significant period of time. In the latter case, the seller may want additional protection due to the length of time that the property will be off the market. The seller's attorney should insist on cash for the down payment. The buyer may wish to use a personal note, but if the buyer defaults, the seller would then have to sue to collect.

The contract of sale should state who will hold the down payment pending the closing. Obviously, the buyer would not be appropriate. The buyer probably will be leery of allowing the seller to retain the money because if the seller defaults, the buyer would then have to sue for the return of the down payment. If a real estate broker is involved, the broker might be the appropriate person to hold the down payment. A broker is generally amendable to doing so. If not, one of the attorneys would be appropriate.

Regardless who holds the down payment, the contract of sale should clearly state what is to be done with the money. Whether the money is to be held for a substantial or short time pending closing, the money should be held in an interest bearing account. The buyer's attorney may want to provide that if the transaction closes, all the interest be applied to the purchase price or at a minimum, the interest be split between the parties. If the seller defaults, the buyer should be entitled to the down payment and all interest earned thereon. In like manner, if the buyer defaults, the seller should retain the earnest money and all interest earned thereon. Some commentators have noted that even in the absence of specification, the seller may retain the down payment when the buyer defaults. Nonetheless, because this is a forfeiture, the seller's attorney is well advised to clearly state in the contract of sale that the seller may retain the down payment upon the default of the buyer. The seller's attorney should also determine whether the seller alone is to retain the down payment on default by the buyer; many form agreements state that the broker is entitled to one-half of the down payment in the event of the buyer's default.

The buyer's attorney should include a provision stating that upon seller's default or other occurrence, such as lack of marketability of title or failure of a condition, the down payment is to be returned to the buyer within a specific period of time. To trigger the time period, the buyer's attorney should provide for notice to the seller upon the failure of a condition.

The seller and buyer should determine whether or not the retention for the return of the down payment is to be the sole remedy available to the non-defaulting party. The seller's attorney may wish to phrase this as a liquidated damages clause; however, due consideration should be given to whether the retention of the down payment is to be the seller's sole remedy. The seller's attorney should consider the sufficiency of the down payment and expressly provide for other remedies such as damages or specific performance. The buyer's attorney, on the other hand, may wish to limit the buyer's liability to the down payment.

VIII. Contingencies

Rarely does a contract for sale not include at least one contingency. Typically, a contingency is requested by the buyer who desires to have time to verify certain subject matters while keeping the seller committed to the sale. The seller, on the other hand, should be concerned with the effect of the contingency and should carefully scrutinize its wording.

Obviously, a contingency should be clearly drafted. Express time limits for the waiver or exercise of the contingency should be included. While the contingency is in effect, the seller typically has the property off the market. If the delay is long, a seller might miss several potential buyers. The seller's attorney therefore should consider one or more of the following drafting alternatives. First, a reasonable time period should be established for exercise or waiver of the contingency. For example, depending upon the custom in the area, a reasonable period of time to determine the status of the title might be three to four weeks. Obviously, mutually agreed upon written extensions are always an alternative. Second, the seller's attorney should consider the possibility of continuing to list the property for sale. The contract of sale could provide that the buyer has a stated period of time, for example, forty-eight hours after receipt of notice from the seller of another bona fide offer, in which the buyer must either waive the contingency or terminate the contract. Alternatively, the contract of sale could permit the seller to continue showing the property and accept other offers as long as the later offers are contingent on the failure of the first offer to close.

Adequate provisions should be included for notice of exercise or waiver of the contingency. The format of the notice should be specified, for example, in writing delivered by mail to the seller. The contract should also state the consequences of lack of receipt of notice by the given date. Typically, failure to give notice results in waiver of the contingency.

. . . .

A. The Financing Contingency

Probably the most common contingency in a contract for sale of residential property is the financing clause. It is a rare buyer who can afford to pay cash. Nonetheless, this clause is too often overlooked or incorrectly drafted. Obviously, the buyer's attorney should make certain that the clause is properly written. It should not be too vague, indefinite, illusory, or, on the other hand, drafted with such excessive detail that it permits a party to escape on mere technicalities. Today, courts tend to utilize a reasonableness standard to compensate for any indefiniteness and a good faith standard if the condition appears illusory. Proper drafting, however, can avoid recourse to the courts.

Prior to the advent of "creative financing," financing, generally, was secured from an institutional lender in the form of a conventional loan or an insured loan. The primary concern was that the financing cause be specific. If a traditional loan is contemplated, the buyer's attorney should include the following terms: the interest rate noting the upper acceptable limits, the loan-to-value ratio noting the minimum ratio, the term noting the minimum or maximum acceptable terms, and the maximum acceptable points or closing costs. The seller's attorney should verify that the specified terms are realistic and should expressly require the wish to include a provision requiring the buyer to approach a stated number of institutions for the financing or, alternatively, the seller to seek financing for the buyer.

B. The contingency for Title Examination

Another common contingency clause in the contract of sale involves the determination of the title's status. In the absence of a clause, a marketable title will be implied. Nonetheless, it is to the advantage of both the seller and buyer to include a clause delineating their respective duties. For example, the seller need not provide a marketable title until the closing date. Obviously, such a time delay could hurt either party; the seller would have the property off the market for a considerable amount of time, and the buyer would not know until he closing whether the title was in fact marketable. Consequently, a provision should be inserted in the contract stating that the determination will be made by a specific date. The time period selected should be shorter than that set for closing, but should conform to local custom and the time restraints required to do an adequate title search. Depending on the particular locality, the determination of marketability of title may be accomplished by a title search based on courthouse records, from a title abstract, or from the files of a title insurance company. The seller or buyer may perform the search or agree to furnish either the abstract of title or title policy for review. Ultimately, it is the buyer who must be satisfied with the status of the title. The seller, nevertheless, should note any exceptions to the marketability of the title in the contract.

If the title proves to be unmarketable, the contract should provide that the seller receive timely written notice stating the alleged defect. The seller should be allowed reasonable time to cure the title defect. The consequences of failure to cure the alleged defect should also be stated in the contract For example, the buyer may want the option either to proceed with the closing, to purchase at a reduced rate, or to terminate the contract. Other remedies might include requiring the seller to bring a quiet title action or to provide title insurance. The contract of sale should state the remedies selected by the parties.

If there is to be time between the title search and the closing, the buyer should include a provision stating that there will be no change in the status of title form the time of the title search and closing. The buyer should also verify that no change has occurred on the date of closing, especially if an escrow closing is not used.

C. Contingency for Inspections

An increasingly popular contingency is to allow for an inspection of the physical premises. Buyers are specially interested in the condition of items such as the plumbing, roof, and furnace. The increased interest coincides with the judicial trend to imply a warranty of habitability to new homes sold by builders. As noted in the implied warranty cases, the use of caveat emptor is no longer applicable in the modern market, at least regarding the sale of new homes by builders, because the modern buyer has neither the requisite expertise to detect problems with the home nor the bargaining power to require express warranties. The implication of this warranty, though expanded in recent years to extend the builder's liability to subsequent buyers, has not been implied for older or used homes. The duty of the buyer to inquire about problems continues to exist although the courts are requiring a greater duty of disclosure by the seller, especially regarding latent defects. The seller's attorney should counsel the seller not to expressly warrant the condition of various items in the home, such as the plumbing or the roof, unless the seller has actual knowledge of their condition. A properly worded contingency for inspection can assist in a smooth transaction by alerting both parties to the importance of the issue of habitability.

The contingency clause should state further that inspections are to be conducted soon after the contact of sale has bene signed. A short item period will limit the period the property is off the market, if the seller is not allowed to continue showing the property. The clause should state who is to perform the inspections, what inspections are to be made, who is to pay for them, when they are to be performed, and what consequences will follow if the inspection reveals a problem. . . .

D. Miscellaneous Contingencies

Depending on the locale and the needs and desires of the contracting parties, other conditions may be included in the contract of sale. For example, in some parts of the country a termite inspection is common even if other inspections are not performed. Another popular contingency allows the buyer to condition the buyer's performance on his ability to sell his present residence. This assures the buyer of the requisite funds needed to purchase the new home and relieves him of the obligation of paying for two homes simultaneously. Sellers, on the other hand, should resist such clauses because they require the seller to remove his home from the market with no assurance of a sale. Possible compromise clauses include: a short period for the contingency to be satisfied or waived, a good faith requirement by the buyer to sell the buyer's existing residence, permitting the seller to continue offering the house for sale subject to the first contract or a combination of these provisions. The buyer could be given the right to exercise or waive the contingency within a stated period of time after notice by the seller of another bona fide offer.

IX. Dates

All dates contained in the contract of sale should be clearly stated. Of great importance is the closing date. The parties should set a realistic closing date, accommodating the time requirements for financing and title searches as well as the particular needs of the parties. For example, a buyer who is moving into the area may have special requirements to coordinate the buyer's move.

The date of possession should be stated. If the contact does not expressly state otherwise, possession will follow the legal title; the buyer will be entitled to possess the house on the closing date.

. . . .

The parties' attorneys should verify whether the dates set in the contract are important to their respective clients. If the closing must occur on a stated date because the money is needed to buy another home or possession is needed to facilitate a move, the contract should state that time is of the essence. Without such a clause, or without it being necessarily implied form the language or conduct of the parties, the court will allow additional reasonable time. The attorney should specify the times to which the provision applies.

. . . .

X. Risk of Loss

No contract for the sale of land would be complete without the inclusion of appropriate provision of the risk of loss which may occur to the property between the signing of the contract and the transfer of title.

. . . .

Most buyers and sellers probably do not realize that the buyer, in the majority of jurisdictions, will bear the risk of loss if the property is destroyed before closing. All parties, particularly buyers, are benefitted by providing for the risk of loss and insurance in the contract of sale. The buyer's attorney will want to keep the risk of loss on the seller until closing or until there is a change in possession. The risk of loss clause should be written to include all losses caused by sudden casualty and those losses that are not the fault of either party.

The procedure to be followed upon the occurrence of a casualty should also be noted in the clause. The seller should be required to notify the buyer, and the clause should specify the relief if a loss occurs. For example, the buyer may wish to have the option to purchase the property with no abatement in the purchase price, with an abatement equal to the insurance proceeds, with an abatement equal to the actual loss sustained, or with the opportunity to terminate the contract. The seller, on the other hand, may wish to limit such options, particularly if the loss is relatively minor. The seller may want the buyer to accept the property with an abatement in the purchase price equal to the insurance or the loss, or the seller may wish to have the opportunity to repair. Only if the loss is substantial should the buyer have the right to terminate.

Concomitant with the risk of loss provisions should be provisions for insurance. Typically, the seller has insurance on the property. The buyer's attorney may wish to provide that the seller continue to carry insurance, and perhaps have it increased to the full purchase price for the benefit of the buyer. The buyer, however, may wish to secure his own insurance. If the seller agrees to carry insurance of the buyer, the seller may want to require the buyer to complete the sale despite a loss.

After having used due care in drafting a risk of loss clause, the seller should also be sure that the protective clause is not negated by other provisions in the contract. The contract of sale often provides that the seller will deliver the property in the same condition, absent normal wear and tear, as it was on the date of signing the contract. The inclusion of such a clause might negate or modify the provisions contained in the risk of loss clause. A careful draftsperson will tie the two provisions together.

XI. Prorations

Provisions should be included in the contract of sale of the prorations of certain ongoing expenses. The most common proration is for real estate taxes. Typically, real estate taxes are prorated to the date of closing. Depending on the area, the current tax bill for the property might not be available. If not, the proration generally is based on the last available tax bill. The contract should provide for the adjustment of proration discrepancies. If the discrepancy is substantial, the parties should consider the use of an escrow. The method of proration may also make a difference. For example, the proration may be based on a 360-day year, a 365-day year, a division into respective six-month time periods, or on tables. If a discrepancy in amounts is possible, the method of proration and adjustment to be used at the closing should be specified in the contract of sale.

A provision for the proration of special tax assessments is commonly appended to prorations of real estate taxes.

. . . .

XIII. Conclusion

The contract of sale is the vital document in the real estate transaction. It requires the ideas and skilled drafting of an attorney. The foregoing suggestions highlight several provisions which should be included in the contract of sale but are often omitted or poorly drafted when the contract of sale is prepared by a layperson or when a form is used. These suggestions can be readily incorporated into a simple contract of sale with appropriate changes depending on the circumstances. The provision are always needed, however, for the protection of both buyers and sellers.

Exercise 26: False Advertising Statute

A portion of the California false advertising law, Calif. Bus. & Prof. Code § 17,500, reads as follows:

> It is unlawful for any person, firm, corporation or association, or any employee thereof with intent directly or indirectly to dispose of real or personal property or to perform services professional or otherwise, or anything of any nature whatsoever or to induce the public to enter into any obligations relating thereto, or make or disseminate or cause to be made or disseminated before the public in this state, or to make or disseminate or cause to be made or disseminated from this state before the public in any state, in any newspaper or other publication, or any advertising device, or by public outcry or proclamation, or in any other manner or means whatever, any statement, concerning such real or personal property or services, professional or otherwise, or concerning any circumstance or matter of fact connected with the proposed performance or disposition thereof, which is untrue or misleading, and which is known or which by the exercise of reasonable care should be known, to be untrue or misleading, or for any person, firm, or corporation to so make or disseminate or cause to be so made or disseminated any such statement as part of a plan or scheme with the intent not to sell such personal property or services, professional or otherwise, so advertised at the price stated therein, or as so advertised.

a. Construct an element-by-element outline of this statute. Make express whatever elements the *such* in lines 17, 26 and 28 incorporate by implication; this will require you to list many of the elements twice.

b. After resolving any ambiguities, uncertainties, and possible mis-translations of probable legislative intent, but without otherwise changing the substance of the statute, draft a revision.

Exercise 27: Attorney's Retainer Agreement

TO: Most Junior Associate

FROM: Most Senior Partner

RE: Retainer Agreement

Attached is a copy of a plaintiff's litigation retainer agreement we have used since my beloved Grandfather founded the firm in 1929. The Executive Committee, in their infantile wisdom, has suggested that we need to revise it -- because of both style and substance. I think otherwise, but in this instance I will bow to their wishes.

You are said to be a reasonably competent drafter. Do something with it.

Time-log this as "Firm Work" and do not let it interfere with your billable hours.

AGREEMENT OF RETAINER AND EMPLOYMENT FOR THE RENDERING OF LEGAL AND RELATED SERVICES

KNOW ALL MEN BY THESE PRESENTS:

This agreement of retainer and employment for the rendering of legal and related services, made this the _____ day of _________, 19__, at __________________, by and between ______________________ who is hereinafter known as "client" and _______________________ of the firm of

Savage, Pillage, and Lute hereinafter known as "attorney," WITNESSETH:

Client employs and retains attorney to represent him as his attorney-at-law in a cause of action against ____________________ regarding ______________________
____
____
____
____
________________________________ and empowers him to effect a compromise in said matter or to institute such legal action as may be advisable in his judgment, and agrees to pay him for his services ____ percent (__%) of the total amount recovered, if said cause of action is settled without the institution of legal action; or ___ percent (__%) of the total amount recovered after suit is filed but before trial on said matter commences; or ___ percent (__%) of the total amount recovered under a verdict and judgment rendered in said matter by a court of competent jurisdiction. In addition, regardless of the outcome of the suit or settlement efforts, client shall be responsible for all costs, expenses, and disbursements.

Attorney is hereby given a lien on the said claim or cause of action, on any sum recovered by way of compromise or settlement, and on any judgment that may be recovered thereon, for the sum and share hereinbefore mentioned, as his fee; and it is further agreed that attorney shall have all general, possessory, or retaining liens, and all special or charging liens known to the common law; and it is further agreed that attorney may retain his share out of the amount finally collected by settlement, suit, or judgment in full of his services rendered.

Client agrees that he will enter into no settlement in said suit except with the prior approval and in the physical presence of attorney, and should he do so in violation of this agreement he agrees to pay attorney the sum and share hereinabove indicated.

Client agrees not to replace said attorney or terminate his services without the consent of attorney, except for misconduct or incapacity of said attorney to act; and if substitution or termination is effectuated in violation hereof, attorney shall be entitled to the full share and sum hereinabove indicated.

It is agreed that attorney has made no guarantees, warranties, or representations regarding the successful consummation or termination of said cause of action, and all expressions relative thereto are matters of opinion only.

Attorney accepts said retainer on the conditions hereinbefore enumerated.

In witness whereof the parties have set their hands and seals on the date first above mentioned.

Redraft the retainer agreement, adding or deleting provisions as necessary. Assume that the Model Rules of Professional Conduct have been adopted in your state. You determine that the following Rules might be relevant to the content of a retainer agreement.

American Bar Association Model Rules of Professional Conduct*

Rule 1.2 Scope of Representation

(a) A lawyer shall abide by a client's decision concerning the objectives of representation . . . and shall consult with the client as to the means by which they are to be pursued. A lawyer shall abide by a client's decision whether to accept an offer of settlement of a matter. . . .

(c) A lawyer may limit the objectives of the representation if the client consents after consultation.

Rule 1.4 Communication

(a) A lawyer shall keep a client reasonably informed about the status of a matter and promptly comply with reasonable requests for information.

(b) A lawyer shall explain a matter to the extent reasonably necessary to permit the client to make informed decisions regarding the representation.

Comment

[1] The client should have sufficient information to participate intelligently in decisions concerning the objectives of the representation and the means by which they are to be pursued, to the extent the client is willing and able to do so. For example, a lawyer negotiating on behalf of a client should provide the client with facts relevant to the matter, inform the client of communications from another party and take other reasonable steps that permit the client to make a decision regarding a serious offer from another party. A lawyer who receives from opposing counsel an offer of settlement in a civil controversy . . . should promptly inform the client of its substance unless prior discussion with the client have left it clear that the proposal will be unacceptable. . . . Even when a client delegates authority to the lawyer, the client should be kept advised of the status of the matter.

[2] Adequacy of communication depends in part on the kind of advice or assistance involved. For example, in negotiations where there is time to explain a proposal, the lawyer should review all important provisions with the client before proceeding to an agreement. . . .

Rule 1.5 Fees

(a) A lawyer's fee should be reasonable. . . .

(c) A fee may be contingent on the outcome of the matter for which the service is rendered, . . . A contingent fee agreement shall be in writing and shall state the method by which the fee is to be determined, including the percentage or percentages that shall accrue to the lawyer in the event of settlement, trial or appeal, litigation and other expenses to be deducted from the recovery, and whether such expenses are to be deducted before or after the contingent fee is calculated. Upon conclusion of a contingent fee matter, the lawyer shall provide the client with a written statement stating the outcome of the matter and, if there is a recovery, showing the remittance to the client and the method of its determination.

Comment

Terms of Payment

. . . .

[3] . . . When there is doubt whether a contingent fee is consistent with the client's best interest, the lawyer should offer the client alternative bases for the fee and explain their implications. Applicable law may impose limitations on contingent fees, such as a ceiling on the percentage.

Rule 1.8 Conflict of Interest: Prohibited Transactions

. . . .

(e) A lawyer shall not provide financial assistance to a client in connection with pending or contemplated litigation, except that:

(1) a lawyer may advance court costs and expenses of litigation, the repayment of which may be contingent on the outcome of the matter; . . .

. . . .

(j) A lawyer shall not acquire a proprietary interest in the cause of action or subject matter of litigation the lawyer is conducting for a client, except that the lawyer may:

(1) acquire a lien granted by law to secure the lawyer's fee or expenses; and

(2) contract with a client for a reasonable contingent fee in a civil case.

Rule 1.16 Declining or Termination Representation

. . . .

(d) Upon termination of representation, a lawyer shall take steps to the extent reasonably practicable to protect a client's interests, such as giving reasonable notice to the client, allowing time for employment of other counsel, surrendering papers and property to which the client is entitled, and refunding any advance payment of fee that has not been earned. The lawyer may retain papers relating to the client to the extent permitted by other law.

Exercise 28: Association By-Laws

TO: Associate

FROM: Partner

IN RE: Lake Bueno Homeowner's Association

A group of homeowners living up on Lake Bueno has retained our firm to assist it in forming a homeowner's association. They will need to form a nonprofit corporation and get tax-exempt status from the IRS. Mr. Rehnquist, of our Tax Department, is working on the application for tax exempt status and Ms. O'Conner, in our General Corporate Department, will file the actual articles of incorporation with the Secretary of State. In both instances, however, they will need to attach a set of by-laws, which I want you to draft.

Lake Bueno is located in northeast McDonald County, on the Travis River. It runs from the dam near Pleasantville up to where the Buckhorn Creek feeds into the river. It is owned by the Consolidated Power Company, which generates power through the dam that forms the lake. Consolidated still owns about a fifth of the land contiginous to the lake. The rest has been divided into lots ranging from half an acre to two acres, which Consolidated has either sold outright or leases (usually 30 years) with an option to buy. The

State maintains three public boat ramps on the lake.

The homeowners apparently have several specific concerns. Consolidated has not been cooperative in warning the homeowners of "draw downs" and its pier, seawall, and riprap permitting process is slow. They also feel that the company has not done enough to fight hydrilla, which is choking several of the shallow coves. And they are real concerned over what Consolidated might want to do with the remaining land it owns and would like to at least have some input on that. Basically, they feel that Consolidated is oblivious to their interests and would like to have a united front in dealing with the company.

The are also concerned about pollution to the lake, specifically Tom's Hog Farm which is twenty miles upriver. They say that runoff from the hog pens is causing a problem and that the State Department of Environmental Control has pretty much ignored their complaints.

The also have complaints with the county -- poor road maintenance, the three trash dumpster areas on the lake are filthy, slow response time by the sheriff, feral dogs running in the woods near the lake, failure to enforce the law against fishing from bridges (which they say causes serious safety problems), and so on.

At the very least, they say, an organization like this can keep the homeowners informed of things that are going on in their community that affect the value of their property and the quality of life on the lake. For example, they would like to put out a monthly newsletter.

Finally, they want an organization that can spearhead all kinds of community programs and events -- a 4th of July boat parade and fireworks display, boating and swimming classes, Crime Watch, road and shore cleanups, and the like.

They want to limit membership to owners and permanent residents of lake front property.

Mr. Rehnquist says to be careful not to suggest that the association will engage in any partisan political activities. Indeed, I think you should have a provision specifically prohibiting it. Ms. O'Connor says that all she needs for incorporation purposes are that the by-laws have a board of directors, an annual meeting for the election of directors, and procedures for dissolution (including disbursement of remaining funds).

a. On the basis of this information, make an outline of the substantive content of your by-laws.

b. Draft the by-laws.

Exercise 29: Simple Will

You have just passed the bar and opened a solo practice. Your former roommate, Edward Edison, who was getting a masters degree in mechanical engineering while you were going to law school, has asked you to draft a *simple will* for him. You remember that Professor Whipple, who taught you Wills & Estates, often said, "There is no such thing as a *simple will*!" However, you believe that Eddie's may be such a will.

What Eddie owns and who he wants it to go to are as follows:

To his brother Thomas:
- A lot at Lake Lurie, North Carolina.
- An 18 foot Lowes bass fishing boat with 60 hp Mercury motor and trailer.
- All his fishing gear.

(If Thomas is not alive when Eddie dies, he wants all this to go to Tom's son, Alva.)

To his nephew Alva (Tom's son, age 5):
- His collection of Batman comics.
- $1,500 to be put into a trust fund payable to Alva when he is 18.
- (If Alva is not alive when Eddie dies, he wants the comics to go to Thomas but the money to revert to the residue of his estate, to be distributed as described below.)

To the Whitfield University College of Engineering:
- His collection of 19th Century mechanical drawings.

To the Mt. Hebron United Methodist Church (Pineview, North Carolina) Soup Cellar Fund: Everything else (currently a Ford Explorer, some furniture, books, TV, stereo, computer, clothing, and other personal items, $500 in a savings account, and about $6,000 in mutual funds) to be liquidated and the money paid over to the Fund (the bequest to Alva should be paid first, out of this money).

He wants Thomas to be his Executor.

Draft a will for Eddie. *See* Child 244-83.

Exercise 30: Requirements Contract

TO: Senior Associate

FROM: Senior Partner

RE: Contract Revision

Once more, I must call upon your expertise as a drafter.

Attached is a contract that was drafted by one of our summer clerks. The substance of the contract accurately reflects the desires of our client, the Sooner Sand Company, but the style and format of the contract are atrocious! I have discovered that the clerk went to this client's file, found a contract my grandfather had drafted for this client back in 1929, and simply changed the dates and some minor details. That will not do.

Ironically, the contract the clerk relied on led to litigation. *McMichael v. Price*, 58 P.2d 549 (Okla. 1936). Although our firm won the case, we should not be producing documents that are even susceptible of provoking litigation. You might read the case to see if you need to do anything to avoid a reoccurrence of that problem.

For the benefit of this hapless clerk: First, prepare a line-by-line critique of the contract. Then draft a revision. This will give the clerk a better idea of the quality work we demand in this law firm.

Contract

This Contract and Agreement entered into on this the 5th day of August, 1998, by and between Harley T. Price III, doing business as the Sooner Sand Company, party of the first part, and Page Peregrinus, party of the second part, witnesseth:

Whereas, the party of the first part is engaged in the business of selling and shipping sand from Tulsa, Oklahoma, to various points in the United States; and,

Whereas, the party of the second part is the owner of a plot of ground hereinafter described as follows, to wit: Lot 65, Section 10, Township 20 North, Range 15 East, Tulsa County; and

Whereas, the party of the first part is desirous of buying and the party of the second part is desirous of selling various grades and qualities of sand from the plot of ground hereinabove described;

Now, THEREFORE, in consideration of the mutual promises herein contained, the said second party agrees to furnish all the sand of various grades and qualities which the first party can sell for shipment to various and sundry points outside of the City of Tulsa, Oklahoma, and to load all of said in suitable railway cars for delivery to said Frisco Railway Company as said initial carrier. Said second party agrees to furnish the quantity and quality of sand at all and various times as the first party may designate by written or oral order, and agrees to furnish and load same within a reasonable time after said verbal or written order is received.

In consideration of the mutual promises herein contained, first party agrees to purchase and accept from second party all of the sand of various grades and quality which the said first party can sell, for shipment to various and sundry points outside the City of Tulsa, Oklahoma, provided that the sand so agreed to be furnished and loaded by the said second party shall at least be equal to in quality and comparable with the sand of various grades sold by other sand companies in the City of Tulsa, Oklahoma, or vicinity. First party agrees to pay and the second party agrees to accept as payment and compensation for Sand so furnished and loaded, a sum per ton which represents sixty percent (60%) of the current market price per ton of concrete sand at the place of destination of said shipment. It is agreed that statements are to be rendered by second party to first party every thirty days; the account is payable monthly by first party with a discount to be allowed by second party of four cents per ton for payment within ten (10) days after shipment of any quantity of sand.

This contract and agreement shall cover a period of ten years from the date hereof, and shall be binding and effective during said period, and shall extend to the heirs, executors, administrators and assigns of both parties hereto.

Dated this 5th day of August, 1999.

____

Sooner Sand Company, by
Harley T. Price III,
Party of the first part.

____

Page Peregrinus,
Party of the second part.